The Comedy of Terrors!

A play

John Goodrum

Samuel French — London
New York - Toronto - Hollywood

© 2005 BY JOHN GOODRUM

Rights of Performance by Amateurs are controlled by Samuel French Ltd, 52 Fitzroy Street, London W1T 5JR, and they, or their authorized agents, issue licences to amateurs on payment of a fee. **It is an infringement of the Copyright to give any performance or public reading of the play before the fee has been paid and the licence issued.**

The Royalty Fee indicated below is subject to contract and subject to variation at the sole discretion of Samuel French Ltd.

> Basic fee for each and every
> performance by amateurs   Code L
> in the British Isles

The Professional Rights in this play are controlled by SAMUEL FRENCH LTD.

The publication of this play does not imply that it is necessarily available for performance by amateurs or professionals, either in the British Isles or Overseas. Amateurs and professionals considering a production are strongly advised in their own interests to apply to the appropriate agents for written consent before starting rehearsals or booking a theatre or hall.

ISBN 0 573 11060 3

The right of John Goodrum to be identified as author
of this work has been asserted by him in accordance with
Section 77 of the Copyright, Designs and Patents Act 1988

Please see page iv for further copyright information

THE COMEDY OF TERRORS!

First produced by Rumpus Theatre Company at Sheringham Little Theatre on 10th October 2003 as part of a national tour with the following cast:

The Smiths Susan Earnshaw
The Joneses John Goodrum

Directed by David Gilbrook
Designed by John B Scattergood
Lighting by Keith Tuttle
Sound recording and design by David Gilbrook
Stage manager and sound operator: James Holmes

COPYRIGHT INFORMATION

(See also page ii)

This play is fully protected under the Copyright Laws of the British Commonwealth of Nations, the United States of America and all countries of the Berne and Universal Copyright Conventions.

All rights including Stage, Motion Picture, Radio, Television, Public Reading, and Translation into Foreign Languages, are strictly reserved.

No part of this publication may lawfully be reproduced in ANY form or by any means — photocopying, typescript, recording (including video-recording), manuscript, electronic, mechanical, or otherwise—or be transmitted or stored in a retrieval system, without prior permission.

Licences for amateur performances are issued subject to the understanding that it shall be made clear in all advertising matter that the audience will witness an amateur performance; that the names of the authors of the plays shall be included on all programmes; and that the integrity of the authors' work will be preserved.

The Royalty Fee is subject to contract and subject to variation at the sole discretion of Samuel French Ltd.

In Theatres or Halls seating Four Hundred or more the fee will be subject to negotiation.

In Territories Overseas the fee quoted above may not apply. A fee will be quoted on application to our local authorized agent, or if there is no such agent, on application to Samuel French Ltd, London.

VIDEO-RECORDING OF AMATEUR PRODUCTIONS

Please note that the copyright laws governing video-recording are extremely complex and that it should not be assumed that any play may be video-recorded for whatever purpose without first obtaining the permission of the appropriate agents. The fact that a play is published by Samuel French Ltd does not indicate that video rights are available or that Samuel French Ltd controls such rights.

CHARACTERS

Jo Smith
Fiona Smith } played by the same actress

Beverley Jones
Vyvian Jones } played by the same actor
Janet Jones

The action of the play takes place on the stage of an empty theatre

Time — the present

All place names should be changed, panto style, according to the location of the performance

For Karen

Also by John Goodrum
published by Samuel French Ltd

Sorry, I Love You ...

ACT I

The stage of a theatre

A set of grand theatre curtains hangs UC. *They do not reach as far as the wings each side, so entrances can be made* L *(from the toilet or dressing-rooms) or* R *(from the street, stage door or dressing-rooms). There is a central gap in the masking behind these curtains (unseen by the audience) which allows characters to enter and exit behind the curtains. Also on stage are a battered old step-stool, some lamps, a rope, a ladder and other theatre fit-up equipment*

When the play begins, Jo Smith, a young woman, is alone on stage. She has a handbag with her

Jo (*calling out*) Hallo?

No reply

Hallo?
Beverley (*voice-over from the back of the auditorium; cheerfully*) Hallo.
Jo (*turning out front, relieved, trying to see who's out there*) Oh. Hallo?
Beverley (*voice-over from off* L; *cheerfully*) Hallo.
Jo (*turning* L, *taken aback*) Oh. (*Slightly more warily*) Hallo?

Beverley suddenly enters R *behind Jo*

Beverley Hallo.
Jo (*jumping*) Oh my God! (*Turning to see Beverley and trying to regain her composure*) Ooh! (*When she has*) Hallo.
Beverley (*holding out his hand*) Jo Smith.
Jo (*shaking his hand, smiling*) How do you do, Mr Smith.
Beverley No. That's you.
Jo It is?
Beverley Isn't it?
Jo Oh. Yes. Of course. I'm sorry. I'm a bit confused. You gave me a bit of a shock. I'm Jo Smith. (*She holds out her hand*) How do you do.
Beverley (*shaking her hand*) Hallo.

A slight pause

Jo Vyvian Jones.

Beverley No, Jo Smith.
Jo No. That's you.
Beverley Me?
Jo Isn't it? I'm supposed to be meeting Vyvian Jones.
Beverley Oh yes. Of course. I'm sorry. You've got me at it now too. I'm Vyvian Jones. (*He holds out his hand*) How do you do.
Jo (*shaking his hand, smiling*) Hallo.

A slight pause

Beverley Actually, I've got a bit of a confession to make.
Jo (*still smiling*) Oh yes?
Beverley Yes.
Jo Go on.
Beverley I'm *not* Vyvian Jones.
Jo Oh. Aren't you?
Beverley No.
Jo Then you must be his assistant. I'm supposed to be meeting him — Vyvian Jones, I mean — the theatre director — here. At two o'clock? For an audition? I had a text from my agent.
Beverley Ah. No. You didn't.
Jo Yes, I did.
Beverley No, you didn't.
Jo I did. (*She gets her mobile phone out of her bag*) Look. It's still on it. (*Reading the text message*) "Two o'clock. Theatre Royal. Vyvian Jones. ——
Beverley I know you got a text.
Jo (*still reading*) — 'Keep Your Hands to Yourself'."
Beverley I never touched you!
Jo (*looking up*) No — that's the name of the play.
Beverley Oh. Yes. Sorry.
Jo I'm auditioning for the maid.
Beverley Ah. No, you're not.
Jo Yes, I am! It's in the text.
Beverley I know.
Jo From my agent.
Beverley No, it's not.
Jo Yes, it is!
Beverley I mean, I know it's in the text. It's just that the text isn't from your agent.
Jo Isn't it?
Beverley No.
Jo Yes it is.
Beverley Did you check the number?
Jo What number?

Act I

Beverley Where the text came from.
Jo No, of course I didn't.
Beverley Well, go on then. Check it now.

Jo checks the message, then looks back to Beverley

Jo It's not from my agent.
Beverley I know.
Jo How do you know?
Beverley Because it's from me.
Jo (*taking this in*) You?
Beverley Yes. Me.
Jo (*after a moment's thought*) Then who the hell are you?

A slight pause

Beverley I'd better be honest with you.
Jo Yes, I think so. If you don't mind.
Beverley I've kept you hanging around long enough.
Jo You certainly have.
Beverley Besides, he'll be here soon.
Jo Who?
Beverley Vyvian.
Jo Vyvian Jones?
Beverley Yes.
Jo Ah. So he is coming then?
Beverley Yes, of course he is.
Jo But then who are you? You still haven't told me.
Beverley I'm his brother.
Jo Vyvian Jones's brother?
Beverley Yes. His brother. His brother Beverley.
Jo (*trying not to be amused*) Beverley? Isn't that a woman's name?
Beverley (*defensively*) Not necessarily.
Jo No, I know. But usually.
Beverley I know.
Jo How embarrassing.
Beverley I know.
Jo Come to think of it, isn't Vyvian a woman's name too?
Beverley Not necessarily.
Jo No, I know. But usually.
Beverley I know.
Jo Not quite so embarrassing for him, though, somehow.
Beverley I know.
Jo Being a theatre director. In a way it makes his name more kind of memorable, doesn't it?

Beverley I know.
Jo (*jokingly*) Don't tell me. I suppose your parents really wanted a girl.
Beverley (*genuinely*) How did you guess?
Jo (*after a moment's thought, amused that her joke is correct*) Wildly.
Beverley Well, you're right. At least, our mother did. She was desperate for a girl. But it was Viv and me who came along first. So our father indulged her. Let her call us a load of half-an'-half names.
Jo Not really fair that, was it?
Beverley Not really, no. But then we're not really a terribly fair family.
Jo So what time is he coming?
Beverley Who?
Jo Your brother.
Beverley Oh. Er ... (*Looking at his watch*) Two-thirty. In about twenty-five minutes.
Jo Then I must get ready. Go to the loo. Tidy my face. For the audition.
Beverley Audition?
Jo The one you texted me about.
Beverley Oh. Yes. Right.
Jo Why did you come through to me direct?
Beverley Well ——
Jo (*going on before he can continue*) Why didn't you go through my agent?

Beverley makes to answer

   Why all this subterfuge?

Beverley makes to answer

   And how did you get hold of my number? You are his assistant, aren't you? Even though you're his brother? (*She pauses for breath*)
Beverley (*getting in as Jo pauses*) Er ... I had to. Nothing to do with your agent. I'll explain. Deviously. And ... no. (*Mentally checking*) Yes, I think that answers them all.
Jo Doesn't really explain anything, though, does it?
Beverley You see, there isn't any audition.
Jo No audition.
Beverley And I'm not Vyvian's assistant.
Jo You're not.
Beverley No.
Jo Right. Is this the moment I should start being scared.
Beverley (*taken aback*) Scared?
Jo Yes. Should I scream now and run away into a darkened room with only one door?
Beverley (*not following this*) One door?

Act I

Jo Which you fill with your huge, menacing silhouette as soon as I've backed myself into a corner.
Beverley (*at a loss for words*) Er ...
Jo You are a professional violator of defenceless women, aren't you? That is why you've lured me here?
Beverley (*relieved*) Oh. No.
Jo Are you sure?
Beverley No. I mean, "Yes, I'm sure". In fact, I'm quite the reverse.
Jo What's the reverse?
Beverley I'm a charity worker, you see. I manage a hostel for unfortunate women.
Jo How are they unfortunate?
Beverley Well, they're down on their luck — you know — and they've had to resort to — Well ...
Jo To prostitution?
Beverley To prostitution. Yes. Exactly. Prostitution — to try and earn a bit of money. Our hostel gives them somewhere to go — for a break now and then — away from the people that control their lives.
Jo The pimps?
Beverley Pimps. Yes. Exactly. If you want to call them that. Because that's what they are. Yes. Away from them.
Jo Isn't that rather dangerous?
Beverley Well ... Yes. Yes, it is. Now and then.
Jo Especially with a name like Beverley.
Beverley I'm known as Bob at the hostel.
Jo Bob.
Beverley It makes things a bit less embarrassing.
Jo I can imagine.
Beverley Exactly.

A slight pause

Jo So?
Beverley So.
Jo Go on. The subterfuge?
Beverley Ah. Yes. Well. It's a bit complicated.
Jo I'm sure. But Vyvian'll be here soon.
Beverley Oh. God. Yes. (*Looking at his watch*) Twenty minutes. Well. You see, I saw you on the television.
Jo (*flattered*) Oh. Did you? Well, thank you. I only had a small part, of course — and the character won't be coming back ...
Beverley I thought you were really terribly good.
Jo Oh. Great. It would've been nice to have a bit more to say, of course.

Beverley I thought you talked quite a lot. For the length of it.
Jo Did you? Well! And it would've been nice to've been shot from the front, of course, instead of over my shoulder at the detective from behind.
Beverley Detective? I seem to remember you being there on your own.
Jo Was I?
Beverley And they showed you from the front all right. Very clearly. Don't you worry about that.
Jo Did they?
Beverley Oh yes. With lots of writing down the screen beside you.
Jo (*light dawning*) Ah.
Beverley "Nought per cent finance for three years," I think it said.
Jo (*coldly*) Yes.
Beverley Amongst other things.
Jo Really?
Beverley Fantastic! I nearly went out and bought one.
Jo Bought what?
Beverley A car. That *was* what you were advertising, wasn't it?
Jo I expect so.
Beverley Except that I've already got one. A car. So I don't really need another one.
Jo No.
Beverley No, I genuinely thought you were excellent.
Jo (*warming a little*) Well. Thank you.
Beverley Perfect ——
Jo Thanks.
Beverley — to do a little *job* for me.
Jo (*cold again*) What *job*?
Beverley You see, I'd like you to impersonate someone for me.
Jo (*heading for the exit*) I think I'm going to go.
Beverley (*stopping her*) No. Please. I'm desperate. And he'll be here soon. (*Looking at his watch*) Sixteen minutes. I need you to persuade him — my brother Vyvian — that I didn't do something.
Jo Didn't do what?
Beverley (*lightly*) Well, you see, Vyvian's got it into his head —somehow — that a little while ago — in a moment of weakness — and on one occasion only, never to be repeated — I took advantage — in a mutual kind of way — and with her full consent — of one of the young women in my care.
Jo (*slowly, and with a rising inflection*) Right. And how, pray, did Vyvian get this foolish notion into his head?
Beverley One of the other young women at the hostel told him so. When he came there to see me one day.
Jo (*after a slight pause*) So?

Act I 7

Beverley So what?
Jo Why does it matter?
Beverley (*outraged*) Why does it matter?
Jo Yes. That your brother thinks that. Why does it matter?
Beverley Well — it could ruin my career. Couldn't it? If it came out.
Jo Could it?
Beverley Without a doubt. Professional misconduct, you see.
Jo I suppose so. But he wouldn't do that, would he? Your brother, I mean. Surely he wouldn't want to ruin your career.
Beverley Oh, wouldn't he!
Jo What about brotherly love?
Beverley Brotherly love, my foot! Listen — Jo — I'll be honest with you ——
Jo Oh, please do be.
Beverley — there's something not very nice about my brother Vyvian.
Jo Oh dear. Is there?
Beverley Yes. He's got something of the night in him.
Jo Something of the night?
Beverley Well, something of the early evening, anyway. Oh, he's a very successful director, I grant you. Maybe that's why he is. He's ruthless, you see.
Jo Ruthless?
Beverley Ruthless. He eats young actresses for breakfast.
Jo (*pooh-poohing the idea*) Oh, come on!
Beverley And not only that, he's also chairman of the Wokingham (*or local town*) and District Sons of Satan Association.
Jo (*shocked*) Oh, my God! Is he really?
Beverley (*enjoying the effect he's having on her*) Oh, yes.
Jo That's terrible.
Beverley I know. God alone knows what despicable hoops he'd've made you jump through if this audition you've come for had been a real one.
Jo D'you think so?
Beverley Undoubtedly. Haven't you heard the stories?
Jo Well — some of them. You never know whether to believe they're true or not.
Beverley Oh, they're true all right! Believe me. As true as my name's Beverley Jones.
Jo God! So he really might try to ruin your career.
Beverley Yes. And not only that, he might tell Cheryl.
Jo Cheryl? Who's Cheryl?
Beverley Cheryl's my girlfriend. Well, fiancée, really. We're due to be married next year.
Jo This is all getting awfully complicated.

Beverley It is, isn't it? (*Looking at his watch*) Ten minutes. I'll explain as quickly as I can.
Jo Go on.
Beverley Two years ago I met this beautiful woman. The most beautiful woman I've ever met in my life. Her name was Cheryl. It still is, actually. There was no need for her to change it. I'm talking rubbish. Of course there wasn't. I'm nervous, you see. This all means quite a lot to me.
Jo (*looking at her watch*) Nine-and-a-half minutes.
Beverley God. Yes. Right. Well. Cheryl fell in love with me. Whoopee! Good! Result! So I introduced her to the family. Including Vyvian. Bad idea. *He* took a shine to her too. And she to him, in a way. Why do women always fall for the rogue?
Jo They don't *always*.
Beverley Well. Long struggle. Us both trying to persuade her. Her trying to decide. Eventually, she chose me.
Jo There you are, you see.
Beverley I don't know why. Brilliant for me, of course. Very happy. Wedding mooted. Next year. When she comes off long hauls.
Jo Long hauls?
Beverley She's an air hostess, actually. Disappears for weeks at a time. Australia. The Far East.
Jo Oh, I see.
Beverley So …
Jo (*looking at her watch*) Seven minutes.
Beverley Right. Well, a couple of months ago a plane she was on got into trouble.
Jo Oh no!
Beverley Crashed on to a remote jungle island in the Pacific. All communications down.
Jo God!
Beverley I know. For days we had no idea where they were. Then a search plane happened to fly over their island and saw them. They'd heard the plane in the distance, you see, and all come out on to what little beach there is there to wave. They wrote in large letters on the sand "All safe" for the plane to see when it came round again. Oh God, I was so relieved.
Jo I should think so.
Beverley But there was nowhere on the island for the plane to land. And the sea was far too rough at that time of year for it to land there either. Or for a boat to get close, for that matter. It was the stormy season, you see. And the tides were all wrong.
Jo God!
Beverley No. So they had lots of time to plan a proper rescue for the first moment the tides were right and the weather had cleared.

Act I

Jo But ... how did they all survive?
Beverley Oh, there was plenty of food growing on the island for them to eat. And coconut milk to drink. We know that, because when the plane flew over a third time they'd scrubbed out the "All safe" and written, "Don't worry. We've got fruit and nuts."
Jo Gosh.
Beverley (*thinking about it for the first time*) Or maybe they just meant they'd salvaged lots of chocolate from the plane. I don't know. Anyway, we know they're all all right because other planes have managed to fly over the island several times since.
Jo And when was the rescue timed for?
Beverley Today.
Jo Today!
Beverley Yes.
Jo God!
Beverley In fact, it's probably happening right at this very moment. I'll be able to speak to Cheryl again by this evening. And so will Vyvian. And as soon as he does, he's threatening to tell her all this other woman told *him*. About me sleeping with one of my women.
Jo I see.
Beverley He's hoping to put Cheryl off me and persuade her back to him.
Jo That's despicable.
Beverley That's Vyvian.
Jo And did you?
Beverley Did I what?
Jo Did you sleep with one of the women in your hostel?
Beverley Um ...
Jo Beverley?
Beverley Well — yes. Yes, I did.
Jo Beverley!
Beverley I was lonely. I was missing Cheryl. She'd been stuck on that island for over a month.
Jo She's your fiancée!
Beverley Oh, it was just a little lapse. We all have them, don't we?
Jo Do we?
Beverley Don't we?
Jo I don't.
Beverley (*impressed*) Then you're a truly remarkable woman.
Jo (*thinking*) I've had lesser lapses, of course.
Beverley Ah.
Jo I wrote rude words in a library book once.
Beverley Really? What was the book?
Jo It was about acting.

Beverley (*whistling, as if the subject is very dubious*) Acting.
Jo It really got on my nerves. Going on and on about how you have to actually *live* a part if you want to play it properly. Immerse yourself in the character. Do tons of research.
Beverley And don't you?
Jo (*scornfully*) No! All you have to do is to learn the lines and remember where you're supposed to stand.
Beverley I see.
Jo Take this maid I was supposed to be auditioning for. Do you think it would help me to make people laugh more when I trip over the cat and show my knickers to the audience if I've worked out what she had for breakfast?
Beverley (*thinking about it*) Well ...
Jo Of course it wouldn't! You can either act or you can't.
Beverley Maybe a more demanding role ... ?
Jo They're all demanding. In different ways. You've either got the knack of becoming someone else, or you haven't.
Beverley You're certainly very passionate about it.
Jo That's why I wrote in the library book. I felt I had to make some kind of protest.
Beverley I see.
Jo I've never slept with a prostitute, though.
Beverley Ah. Well. Who's to say which lapse is greater? Is it the man who steals a penny? Or the man who steals a pound? Isn't the impulse to do it just the same?
Jo No. I don't think it necessarily is.
Beverley (*carrying on regardless*) So what I thought was: if I happened to meet Vyvian when he comes here for a production meeting at two-thirty (*looking at his watch*) — three minutes! — I should've got you here for one forty-five! — if I happened to meet him here then to talk it over — and if I could have someone here with me to pretend to be this woman he thinks I slept with, then it would be more convincing coming from her lips that we hadn't actually done anything.
Jo What a cheek! Why do you think I'd be any good at playing a prostitute?
Beverley Well, you're an actress, aren't you?
Jo Oh, lovely! I thought the days had long gone when people thought all actresses had no morals.
Beverley (*disappointedly*) Oh. Have they?
Jo Yes! They have!
Beverley Look! I didn't mean that. You'll be brilliant, I know. Just look on it like any other acting job.
Jo But I'm not very good at improvisation.
Beverley Please. Please do it. I'm desperate. I know I shouldn't've done what I did but I did and I love Cheryl so much I just couldn't bear the thought of her finding out and then leaving me and ending up with Vyvian.

Act I

Jo Well...
Beverley And if I'm honest...
Jo (*suspiciously*) Yes?
Beverley If I'm *really* honest...
Jo (*suspiciously*) Yes?
Beverley There's another reason why you'd be just right for this part.
Jo (*suspiciously*) Go on?
Beverley This woman I slept with...
Jo Yes?
Beverley This prostitute...
Jo Yes?
Beverley Well — the woman who gave the game away actually pointed her out to Vyvian. So he knows exactly what she looks like.
Jo So I don't understand. How can *I* pretend to be *her*?
Beverley (*after the slightest of pauses*) It was your sister.
Jo My sister!
Beverley Your twin sister. Fiona. You look just like her.
Jo Fiona's a cow!
Beverley (*taken aback*) Is she?
Jo She's our black sheep.

Beverley is puzzled for a moment

Beverley (*having thought about it*) She was a bit of an animal, I remember that clearly enough.
Jo Fiona! I bet she led you on.
Beverley Well... I think I'd be lying if I said ——
Jo (*interrupting*) She's a monster! She left home when she was fifteen, you know. She was totally uncontrollable. My mother and father were distraught.
Beverley Were they?
Jo That's over ten years ago now.
Beverley Of course.
Jo We could all see exactly the way she was going.
Beverley To the bad?
Jo No. To the bus stop. You can see it just down the road from our front door. She said she was sick of the house. And sick of the street. And sick of the neighbourhood. She just wanted to get away.
Beverley So she came down here.
Jo Yes. Mum and Dad got snippets of news now and then. A phone call every few months or so. The odd note.
Beverley She didn't cut herself off completely, then?
Jo She's never spoken to me.
Beverley Really?
Jo And I've certainly never spoken to her.
Beverley Perhaps you should.

Jo Me? Why?
Beverley Break the ice.
Jo After the way *she's* behaved?
Beverley Why not?
Jo No fear! She even sent Dad one of her business cards once.
Beverley Heavens!
Jo Yes! Nearly gave him a heart attack!
Beverley Right!
Jo I think she was just showing off. Showing us what a rebel she was.
Beverley (*looking at his watch*) It's thirty seconds to half-past two. Will you do it?
Jo Yes. I will.
Beverley (*trying to hug Jo*) I love you!
Jo (*stopping him*) Hey!
Beverley You're a life-saver!
Jo Just a minute.
Beverley What?
Jo You said treat it like any other acting job. Does that mean you're going to pay me?
Beverley Oh.
Jo If I'm doing a job, I should get paid.
Beverley How much do you want?
Jo Oh, you'll have to speak to my agent about that.
Beverley Right. Who's your agent?
Jo Susan Montague.
Beverley (*getting out his mobile phone*) What's her number?
Jo 0207 ——
Beverley (*putting the mobile away*) No! Look! (*Looking at his watch*) Fifteen seconds. Can we discuss this later?
Jo OK. If you like.
Beverley Great!
Jo But — isn't it going to be a bit embarrassing?
Beverley How do you mean?
Jo Well — talking to Vyvian about you know what with loads of other people around for a production meeting?
Beverley Oh, I put all the others off.
Jo Did you?
Beverley Yes, I texted them.
Jo You're quite handy with that mobile phone, aren't you?
Beverley Getting so. Listen. I don't think I can face Vyvian myself.
Jo What?
Beverley I'll get too angry. Hit him or something. Give the whole game away. Can you do it on your own?

Act I

Jo Beverley!
Beverley Please? I'll hide behind this curtain. (*He indicates the theatre curtains* UC) Come out if I need to.
Vyvian (*voice-over, off* R) Bloody hell! You'd think someone could at least put the lights on!
Beverley There he is now! I'm off!
Jo Beverley!
Beverley You'll know it's him because he always sports a red handkerchief in his jacket pocket.
Jo Red handkerchief.
Beverley Oh yes. And of course he looks exactly like me. We're identical too.
Jo Oh my God!
Beverley (*trying to imitate Vyvian's look*) But with a bit of a wicked glint in his eye!
Vyvian (*voice-over, off* R) Where the bloody hell *is* everybody?
Beverley You came tarty for the audition. That's good.
Jo You're outrageous.
Beverley I'm beginning to enjoy it!
Jo Look, you can't just leave me alone with him.
Beverley Oh yes, I can.
Jo He's a devil-worshipper, for God's sake!
Beverley Only on a Sunday. I'll be behind here if you need me. (*He goes to the curtain*) Don't panic!

Beverley exits behind the curtain

Jo (*to herself, in a little voice*) Help!

Vyvian enters R, *dressed identically to Beverley, but with a red handkerchief in his breast pocket. He is very angry*

Vyvian If I'm called for a meeting at two-thirty I bloody expect the bloody meeting to be at bloody two-thirty! (*He sees Jo and stops in his tracks*)

Jo shifts a little, trying to look as she thinks a prostitute should

(*Rakishly, obviously taken with Jo*) Hallo.
Jo (*at length, in a cod cockney accent*) 'Allo. (*After a slight pause she starts chewing imaginary gum*)
Vyvian (*taking a step towards Jo*) Do I know you?
Jo (*still cockney, still chewing; nervously*) I don't know.
Vyvian You seem familiar.
Jo (*sidling towards him, trying to be seductive*) Oh, I am. Very familiar.
Vyvian (*trying to grab her; lecherously*) I say!

Jo (*stepping back; nervously*) But not that familiar!
Vyvian (*moving towards her*) Don't be nervous, my dear.
Jo (*backing away; nervously*) It's not a Sunday, you know.

During the following, Vyvian follows Jo as she backs away

Vyvian Isn't it?
Jo No, it's a Friday.
Vyvian I know.
Jo So there!
Vyvian I don't quite follow you.
Jo (*watching Vyvian follow her*) You could've fooled me.
Vyvian (*stopping in his tracks*) I'm sure I've seen you somewhere before.
Jo (*also stopping, a bit away from Vyvian*) Maybe.
Vyvian Was it on page three?
Jo Page free?
Vyvian Of the *Sun*.
Jo The "Bracknell (*or local town*) News" maybe.
Vyvian Stop teasing me. Give me a clue.
Jo OK then. What about when you was visiting your bruvver.
Vyvian My brother?
Jo At his work.
Vyvian Beverley?
Jo Beverley.
Vyvian (*correcting himself*) I mean Bob.
Jo Bob?
Vyvian Isn't he called Bob?
Jo He's *your* bruvver.
Vyvian He's called Bob — at work.
Jo I know he is. That's where you've seen me.
Vyvian (*recognition dawning*) Of course! You're the one.
Jo Am I?
Vyvian Oh yes!
Jo What one?
Vyvian The one he did it with.
Jo Did he?
Vyvian Fiona. Fiona Smith.
Jo (*chewing nonchalantly*) That's me.
Vyvian You're the one he had his wicked, wicked way with — while his poor defenceless fiancée is far away and unknowing on an idyllic tropical island.
Jo Lucky 'er.
Vyvian But not for long.
Jo No?

Act I 15

Vyvian Oh no! She won't be unknowing for long. By tonight she'll know the whole sorry story.
Jo What story's that, then?
Vyvian I think you know very well, young woman.
Jo (*with a shrug*) Don't fink so. 'Elp me out a bit.
Vyvian Oh, don't play the innocent with me.
Jo (*trying to look innocent*) What?
Vyvian I've never seen anyone look less innocent in my whole life.
Jo Well, I am!
Vyvian Oh, come on! Are you seriously trying to tell me that a few weeks ago you didn't indulge in a romantic conjugation with my brother?
Jo (*blankly*) You what?
Vyvian My brother Beverley — er, Bob.
Jo I don't know what you're talking about.
Vyvian That you didn't get to know him in a thoroughly Biblical sense?
Jo Oh, I've got to know 'im very well indeed.
Vyvian Aha!
Jo Ever since I come to the 'ostel.
Vyvian You see!
Jo But I've never been to church, though.
Vyvian (*puzzled*) What?
Jo (*explaining*) You talking about the Bible.
Vyvian Good God, woman! I know all about it!
Jo Very religious, are you? Read it from cover to cover?
Vyvian No! I mean I know you did it with my brother a few weeks ago!
Jo Did what?
Vyvian Went to bed with him!
Jo (*outraged*) Ooooh! I never!
Vyvian Yes, you did! I've been told all about it!
Jo I'd never take advantage of Bob. Dear, kind, generous, philanfropic Bob!
Vyvian (*sarcastically*) Oh, really!
Jo 'E's a saint, your bruvver Bob is. 'E changed my life for me. 'E turned me right around.
Vyvian I can quite believe he did that!
Jo Anyone 'oo tells you different is a liar.
Vyvian A liar?
Jo Yeah, a liar!
Vyvian Is that so!
Jo 'Oo's the liar?
Vyvian What?
Jo 'Oo's the unreliable lying person 'oo told you that wicked, wicked lie? God! What a lie it is! What a lie! (*Getting a bit carried away*) It's a lie, I tell ya! A wicked, wicked lie! 'Oo's the wicked liar 'oo told you that wicked, wicked lie?

Vyvian (*a little bemused by this outburst*) A young woman at your hostel.
Jo What's 'er name? What's the liar's name? Go on. Tell me! Tell me!
Vyvian Er ...
Jo Tell me the liar's name!
Vyvian I don't know her name.
Jo Don't know it?
Vyvian She didn't tell me.
Jo Didn't she indeed!
Vyvian No.
Jo Was she quite — you know — was she quite ...? (*She pauses for Vyvian to fill in the details*)
Vyvian (*helping her out*) Tall.
Jo (*jumping in*) Tall! Yes! And with ... and with ...? (*She pauses again*)
Vyvian Dark curly hair.
Jo Dark curly hair! I thought so! That's Gabby.
Vyvian Gabby?
Jo Yes, Gabby. Gabby Dribber.
Vyvian Gabby Dribber?
Jo Oh, I might've known! Old Gabby Dribber! She's always making things up, you know.
Vyvian Really?
Jo Oh, yeah! She's a right old trouble maker, she is. Old Fibber Dribber, we call 'er. On account of all the lies she tells.
Vyvian Is that so!
Jo Old Gabby Fibber Dribber. Old Shabby Gabby Fibber Dribber! She's a bit on the large side, ain't she?
Vyvian A little, I suppose.
Jo Yeah! Old Dodgy Podgy Shabby Gabby Fibber Dribber! What made you want to go and believe anything *she* told ya?
Vyvian I saw no reason to doubt her.
Jo Oh, no! And it suited your purposes, no doubt. I've 'eard all about you from Beverley ... Bob!
Vyvian (*relishing his reputation*) Oh! So you've heard all about me, have you?
Jo I most certainly have.
Vyvian And what exactly have you heard all about?
Jo I've heard all about you and Bob's fiancée.
Vyvian (*derisively*) His fiancée!
Jo That's right. 'Is fiancée, Charlotte.
Vyvian His fiancée's called Cheryl.
Jo Whatever. All about 'ow you're going to tell lies about 'im to Cheryl to try and steal 'er away from 'im.
Vyvian It wouldn't be stealing. She fancies me, anyway.

Act I

Jo 'Ow can you do it to 'im? What about bruvverly love?
Vyvian Brotherly love, my eye! All's fair in love and the theatre, my dear. (*With a wicked glint in his eye*) And I'll do anything to get Cheryl away from him.
Jo (*a little nervously*) Anything?
Vyvian (*advancing slowly on Jo*) Yes. Absolutely anything! And I know quite a lot of things to do, believe me!
Jo (*backing away*) I'm sure you do.
Vyvian (*still advancing*) You don't think the fact that you didn't really sleep with him — if, indeed, you didn't ... You don't think that would stop me from telling Cheryl that you did, do you?

During the following, Jo backs away and Vyvian continues to advance

Jo Wouldn't it?
Vyvian Oh, no, my dear! There's a lot about me you don't know, I can tell you!
Jo Oh, yeah?
Vyvian How I deal with young women who come to work for me in the theatre, for instance.
Jo Actresses, you mean.
Vyvian And stage managers, yes.
Jo Them as well. Blimey!
Vyvian But more importantly ...
Jo Yeah?
Vyvian More importantly, I could tell you ...
Jo Yeah?
Vyvian I could tell you — what I do on Sundays!
Jo Oh my Gawd!
Vyvian (*stopping in his tracks*) Just a minute!
Jo (*calling out*) Help!
Vyvian What are you doing here?
Jo Help! (*Suddenly realizing what he's said, and stopping as well*) I beg your pardon?
Vyvian I said, "What are you doing here?"
Jo (*forgetting the cockney accent for a moment*) What am I doing here? (*Correcting herself*) I mean, wot am I doing 'ere?
Vyvian In the theatre.
Jo In the theatre?
Vyvian Yes. What are you doing here? In the theatre?
Jo (*after a pause, having failed to think of a reason*) You may well ask!
Vyvian You're nothing to do with the theatre. Why are you here?
Jo (*off the top of her head*) I came to find Beverley.

Vyvian Beverley?
Jo Bob!
Vyvian Bob!
Jo That's right.
Vyvian But Bob's not here.
Jo Ain't 'e?
Vyvian Why would Bob be here?
Jo 'E said 'e was coming.
Vyvian Coming here?
Jo 'E said so.
Vyvian Why was he coming here?
Jo To talk to you, 'e said. To try and persuade you not to call Charlotte.
Vyvian Cheryl.
Jo Cheryl!
Vyvian (*after a slight pause*) So Bob's come here, has he?
Jo Apparently.
Vyvian To try and talk me round.
Jo Exactly.
Vyvian And you've come here to find Bob, have you?
Jo Yes, I have.
Vyvian Why?
Jo (*after a slight pause*) "Why?"
Vyvian Yes. Why?
Jo (*thinking desperately, then coming out with it*) Because the 'ostel's on fire.
Vyvian On fire!
Jo Yeah! I must find 'im! 'E needs to come back at once! 'Ave you seen 'im?
Vyvian No. No, I haven't.
Jo Then I must look for 'im! I must look everywhere. 'Ere I go. I'm looking. Everywhere! (*Making a show of looking for Bob*) Bob? Bob? Bob? Bob?

Jo exits behind the curtain, calling as she goes, her tone changing when she finds out Beverley isn't there

(*Off*) Bob? (*Calling out genuinely to find him, her voice getting more distant*) Bob? Bob? Bob? Bob?

A very slight pause. Vyvian is a little confused. Then he turns out front

Vyvian (*to himself, derisively*) Bob!
Fiona (*off, calling; her accent is not a lot different from Jo's, just a little harder perhaps*) Bob? Bob?

Fiona enters. She is dressed only very slightly differently to Jo

Act I   19

   Bob?

Vyvian turns to see Jo

   (*Seeing Vyvian*) Oh! there you are!
Vyvian (*suspiciously*) Fiona?
Fiona Hallo.
Vyvian Did you find him?
Fiona Who?
Vyvian Bob.
Fiona (*pulling a jokey face at him, as if he's an idiot*) Well ... yeah!
Vyvian That was very quick of you.
Fiona Was it?
Vyvian Have you said?
Fiona Said what?
Vyvian About the fire.
Fiona What fire?
Vyvian The fire you just told me about.
Fiona Did I?
Vyvian At the hostel.
Fiona I told you at the hostel about a fire?
Vyvian No! You told me about a fire at the hostel!
Fiona What's the difference?
Vyvian The hostel's on fire!
Fiona (*shocked*) Is it?
Vyvian Yes! You just told me!
Fiona (*less shocked*) No, I didn't.
Vyvian Yes, you did!
Fiona I couldn't've done. I've only just found you.
Vyvian Found me?
Fiona Why are you acting so strangely, Bob?
Vyvian And what's happened to your cockney accent? (*Suddenly realizing*) Bob?
Fiona What cockney accent?
Vyvian *I'm Bob?*
Fiona (*pulling her silly face again*) Der!
Vyvian (*grasping the wicked advantages of the situation*) I'm Bob!
Fiona I know you are! I haven't got a cockney accent.
Vyvian I thought you did.
Fiona I put it on occasionally.
Vyvian Do you?
Fiona For the clients.
Vyvian (*knowingly*) Oh!

Fiona Some of them seem to like it.
Vyvian It takes all sorts, I suppose.
Fiona You know that.
Vyvian Do I?
Fiona Of course you do, Bob!
Vyvian Oh, yes. Of course I do, Bob!
Fiona What's all this about a fire?
Vyvian (*helplessly*) I don't know.
Fiona I had to come and find you.
Vyvian Did you?
Fiona Away from the hostel. I hope you don't mind.
Vyvian Why should I mind?
Fiona You said you'd be here.
Vyvian I did?
Fiona I overheard you. Telling one of the others. Before you went out.
Vyvian Oh, I see.
Fiona You seem to've been avoiding me lately.
Vyvian Have I?
Fiona Ever since we — well — you know.
Vyvian Ever since we what?
Fiona You know!
Vyvian No, I don't!
Fiona You can't've forgotten?
Vyvian Can't I?
Fiona (*almost to herself, meaning it*) It was so perfect, wasn't it! So beautiful. So different from any time before.
Vyvian Oh ... You mean — when we ...

Fiona looks at Vyvian

When we ...
Fiona (*pulling her silly face again*) Der!
Vyvian So we *did*, did we?
Fiona (*relishing the memory*) Oh yes, we did!
Vyvian But I thought you just told me ... I mean, I thought you just told — not me — but ...
Fiona Who?
Vyvian Someone else.
Fiona Told someone else what?
Vyvian That we didn't do anything at all.
Fiona Oh no! I'd never tell anyone else that.
Vyvian Wouldn't you?
Fiona No. I'd never tell anyone else anything about it at all.

Act I

Vyvian Really?
Fiona Well, you asked me not to, didn't you?
Vyvian Did I? I mean, yes ... Yes, I did ask you not to, didn't I?
Fiona (*putting her arms around him*) It's our little secret.
Vyvian (*with a wicked gleam*) Oh, yes. So it is! Our little secret!
Fiona And, if anyone did ask me anything about it, I'd just say it never happened like you told me to.
Vyvian What a good girl you are!
Fiona I wish we could tell someone, though.
Vyvian Do you?
Fiona I wish we could tell everyone.
Vyvian Ooh! Now! We don't want it getting into the wrong hands, do we?
Fiona I suppose not.
Vyvian Vyvian's for example.
Fiona Vyvian's?
Vyvian Precisely.
Fiona Who's Vyvian?
Vyvian (*stung*) Who's Vyvian!
Fiona Yes.
Vyvian What do you mean, "Who's Vyvian?"
Fiona You've never mentioned any Vyvian before.
Vyvian Haven't I?
Fiona Who is she?
Vyvian (*outraged*) *She?*
Fiona Yes. Who's this Vyvian?
Vyvian She's my brother!
Fiona What?
Vyvian I mean, *he's* my brother.
Fiona Funny name for a bloke.
Vyvian No, it's not. It's distinguished.
Fiona If you say so.
Vyvian I do.
Fiona I didn't know you had a brother.
Vyvian Didn't you?
Fiona It's news to me.
Vyvian You mean Bob ... I mean, *I* — never mentioned Vyvian to you?
Fiona I don't think so.
Vyvian (*exploding*) Well, who the bloody hell did you think you were talking to just now, then?
Fiona Just now?
Vyvian Yes! Before you met *me* — *me, Bob*, I mean.
Fiona Before I met you?
Vyvian Yes! Just now! Who do you think you were talking to?

Fiona Oh! You mean the bloke I was talking to just now before I came round here and met you.
Vyvian Yes! That's the one. Don't you think he looked just a little bit like me?
Fiona (*putting her head on one side; doubtfully*) Well — *a little* bit, I suppose.
Vyvian Of course, *he's* more handsome.
Fiona Is he?
Vyvian The man you were just talking to.
Fiona I'm not sure about that.
Vyvian Oh, much more! More dashing — and — exciting — and — wicked!
Fiona (*doubtfully*) The bloke I was talking to just now?
Vyvian That's right. Don't you see? That was my brother!
Fiona (*bewildered*) Was it?
Vyvian My wicked brother Vyvian.
Fiona Your wicked brother Vyvian works in a sandwich shop?
Vyvian (*after a slight pause; trying to take this in*) What?
Fiona In the sandwich shop over the road? I was waiting in there, you see? By the window. Watching for you to come in here. I saw you come in, finished my cappuccino, and went to pay the man. He asked me if I'd enjoyed it. I said it was all right. He looks *a bit* like you, I suppose. If you squint.
Vyvian That's not my brother!
Fiona I thought you just said it was!
Vyvian Vyvian doesn't work in a sandwich shop! He's an extremely brilliant and successful theatre director!
Fiona All right! I'm only repeating what you said!
Vyvian Why in God's name did you think Bob would ... I mean, *I* would be coming to this theatre anyway?
Fiona I didn't really think about it. I just heard you say you were coming here and thought it'd be a good chance to get you on your own.
Vyvian Hell's bells!
Fiona You're behaving very strangely, Bob. Have you been drinking or something?
Vyvian I shall be very soon, if this goes on.
Fiona You're usually much quieter than this. Much more ordinary.
Vyvian Yes. A bit dull as well, sometimes, I expect.
Fiona Well ... Just a bit — but then I quite like that!
Vyvian (*in disbelief*) You like it when I'm dull?
Fiona I'm sick of exciting! Because exciting never really is "exciting", is it?
Vyvian Isn't it?
Fiona Not as far as I can see, no. "Exciting" always seems to end up being just plain nasty.

Act I

Vyvian (*getting back to the subject*) You have absolutely no recollection of talking to my identical brother Vyvian just now, do you? Here, on this very stage, ten seconds before you came round that curtain and started talking to me?
Fiona No. I told you. I came straight here from the sandwich shop over the road.
Vyvian Well, *I* was talking to someone who looked exactly like *you* just now. She went off there (*he points*) and you came on there (*he points*).
Fiona I'm losing track of this a bit.
Vyvian You're not the only one!
Fiona Unless it was Jo.
Vyvian Jo?
Fiona My sister.
Vyvian You have a sister Jo?
Fiona You know I have.
Vyvian Do I?
Fiona Of course you do. I've told you all about her. How much she hates me.
Vyvian Oh, yes. Of course you have. And she looks like you, does she?
Fiona Exactly. We're twins. We're identical. I've told you.
Vyvian But what would she be doing here?
Fiona (*as if Vyvian's an idiot*) Well — this is a theatre. She is an actress.
Vyvian (*taking this in*) Oh, yes, of course! She is an actress!
Fiona Perhaps she's got a job here. Not that she'd tell me.
Vyvian Oh, no. She hasn't got a job here.
Fiona How would you know?
Vyvian (*quickly*) I wouldn't! So you've mentioned your sister to me — I mean, me, Bob — before, have you?
Fiona You know I have.
Vyvian And you've told me she's an actress?
Fiona (*pulling a face, stretching out the word*) Y-e-s! I think you're losing your marbles.
Vyvian On the contrary, my dear. I think I've just found them.
Fiona (*confused*) Found your marbles?
Vyvian Don't go away.
Fiona I'm not going to.
Vyvian Stay right here. I've just got to — go and find *Vyvian*. And see if the other people at his production meeting have gone straight to the office.
Fiona Oh, yeah?
Vyvian I'll be right back. This is all most interesting!

Vyvian dashes off R

Fiona (*calling after him*) But ... Bob! I haven't said what I came here to say, yet. Come back! Please! I've got so much to say.

Beverley appears round the L of the UC curtain

Beverley (*in an exaggerated whisper*) How did it go?
Fiona (*jumping, and turning to Beverley*) How did you get round there?
Beverley Sorry I popped off.
Fiona You weren't long.
Beverley Wasn't I?
Fiona Very quick.
Beverley I'm glad it seemed so. Call of nature, you see. I'm a bit worked up and nervous. Always goes straight to my bladder.
Fiona I know. You're always in there.
Beverley Did he swallow it?
Fiona Who?
Beverley Just now.
Fiona Swallow what?
Beverley That you were Fiona.
Fiona I am Fiona.
Beverley No you're not.
Fiona Yes I am!
Beverley Oh, I see!
Fiona See what?
Beverley You're trying it out, are you?
Fiona Trying what out?
Beverley I thought you said you didn't need to.
Fiona Didn't need to what?
Beverley Live the part.
Fiona What are you talking about?
Beverley Actually work out what you've had for breakfast.
Fiona I know what I had for breakfast!
Beverley Oh, well done!
Fiona What?
Beverley I'm sure it'll help.
Fiona Of course I know what I had for breakfast. So do you.
Beverley Do I?
Fiona Well, you were sitting there with me.
Beverley Well — in real life, yes.
Fiona You and all the others. You had toast and peanut butter and I had "Choco Crunchies" — without the milk
Beverley This is frighteningly accurate.
Fiona It was only this morning, you know. Do you think my memory's going or something?
Beverley (*after a slight pause, taking this in, looking at her*) Ah. You are actually Fiona, aren't you?

Act I   25

Fiona Well — hallo!
Beverley (*panicking*) You're Fiona!
Fiona Bob ...
Beverley (*slightly frantically*) What're you doing here?
Fiona I've just told you.
Beverley Have you?
Fiona I think you really are losing your marbles.
Beverley What marbles?
Fiona The marbles you said you'd found.
Beverley (*helplessly*) Help!
Fiona Look! Let me tell you what I've come here to tell you.
Beverley What's that?
Fiona I love you!
Beverley (*horrified*) No, you don't!
Fiona (*indignantly*) Yes, I do! Don't you tell me whether I love you or not! I know how I feel.
Beverley You can't do.
Fiona Oh, yes, Bob. I can.
Beverley Fiona ...
Fiona My life's been so horrible up to now. Not at all like I thought it would be.
Beverley (*trying to be sympathetic, but wanting all this over with*) Oh dear.
Fiona I wanted to be on my own.
Beverley Good idea! Off you go.
Fiona (*ignoring him*) Independent. In charge of myself. But I never have been. I've always been answerable to someone else. Mum and Dad. The Social. Men who bought me. Pimps who owned me.
Beverley (*sympathetically*) Fiona ...
Fiona And then I met you.
Beverley So you did.
Fiona I liked you from the start.
Beverley Did you?
Fiona You're so — handsome.
Beverley (*liking this*) Oh. Do you think so?
Fiona Yes.
Beverley (*liking this*) Oh!
Fiona Whatever the other girls say.
Beverley (*deflated*) Oh.
Fiona And then when we ... well ... like I said.
Beverley (*worried*) When did you say?
Fiona (*moving close to Beverley*) It was so wonderful! So — right! I was involved, for once! I wasn't just being used.
Beverley Fiona ... ?

Fiona (*putting her arms around him*) So what I want to say is — can't we go on? Please? You and me? Together? Can't we? Can't we become a couple — like real people do?
Beverley (*warming to her*) Fiona ...
Fiona You do love me too, don't you?
Beverley (*trying to be honest*) Well ...
Fiona (*breaking away*) Oh, please, you must! If this doesn't work out, I think I'm going to top myself!
Beverley No! You mustn't do that! Whatever happens!
Fiona (*becoming tearful*) You don't love me, do you?
Beverley Fiona ...
Fiona That's why you've been avoiding me ever since we did it. I didn't want to think it — because of how I felt.
Beverley Fiona, I can't be with you.
Fiona (*in floods*) Please.
Beverley I can't.
Fiona (*through her tears*) Why not?
Beverley Because I'm engaged to somebody else.

Fiona wails

I'm in love with somebody else.

Fiona wails again

I'm sorry. It was a mistake.
Fiona Is that all I am? A mistake?
Beverley Yes. I mean, no! It was nice. Wasn't it? But not for all time. Just for once.
Fiona (*through her tears, angrily*) Oh, I promised myself I'd never get involved! Why have I got myself involved! You're just like all the others! Except you had your shag for free!
Beverley Fiona!
Fiona (*moving towards the wings, still sobbing*) Don't go! I haven't finished this yet! I've got a lot more I want to get off my chest! But I must just ... (*breaking down*) ... I can't ... Ooooooh!

Fiona runs off in floods of tears

Beverley (*calling after her*) Fiona! Come back! Let me explain! Don't do anything silly! Fiona!

Beverley moves to follow Fiona off

Act I 27

Jo appears on the other side of the stage

Jo Beverley?
Beverley (*stopping and turning to look at her*) Oh!
Jo No red hankie. Beverley!
Beverley Jo?
Jo Who else?
Beverley Not Fiona?
Jo Fiona?
Beverley Yes.
Jo Why would I be Fiona?
Beverley Because she's here.
Jo Here!
Beverley She's just run out. In floods of tears.
Jo Fiona's here?
Beverley Yes! To tell me how much she loves me.
Jo God! Has Vyvian seen her?
Beverley I don't know.
Jo Because if he has, then he'll have worked out about *me* — probably.
Beverley Worked out what?
Jo That I wasn't her — when I met him just now.
Beverley Oh. Yes, of course! How did it go?
Jo Not good.
Beverley Oh Lord!
Jo He believed me that we didn't do anything ——
Beverley (*brightening*) Oh!
Jo — but he said he was going to tell Charlotte we did anyway.
Beverley Who's Charlotte?
Jo Your fiancée.
Beverley My fiancée's called Cheryl.
Jo That's who I said. Cheryl.
Beverley No, you didn't.
Jo Whatever!
Beverley He's going to tell Cheryl anyway?
Jo That's what I just said.
Beverley (*in desperation*) Aaaagh!
Jo I'm off, then.
Beverley Off? Off where?
Jo If Vyvian finds out I'm not really Fiona, then he might try to do to me today what he usually does on Sundays even though it's only a Friday.
Beverley Well, yes, that's true. He might.
Jo So. Bye, then. It's been lovely!
Beverley You did your best. Thank you.

Jo Any time. (*She turns to go, but then turns back*) No. Actually, I don't mean that. Never again!
Beverley Right! Fair enough!
Jo I'll see you. (*She turns to go, but then turns back*) No. Wait. My money.
Beverley Money?
Jo You were going to pay me.
Beverley Oh. Yes.
Jo I played the part all right, didn't I? I convinced him I was Fiona. It's not my fault he's a despicable bastard who's going to tell Charlotte ——
Beverley Cheryl.
Jo —— Cheryl that you and Fiona did it anyway.
Beverley No. No, that's not your fault.
Jo So I should still get paid.
Beverley I'll call your agent.
Jo I'll give you her number.
Beverley Don't bother. I can look it up.
Jo Hang on!
Beverley What?
Jo How did you get hold of my mobile number in the first place?
Beverley Ah. Yes.
Jo Well?
Beverley Deviously. If I'm honest.
Jo (*having waited a split second for him to go on on his own*) Go on.
Beverley I had a sneak look in your sister's bag when she wasn't looking. And found her address book.
Jo Fiona's got my mobile number in her address book?
Beverley Well, yes. That's how I found it.
Jo She's never called me.
Beverley Hasn't she?
Jo She must've got it from Mum and Dad.
Beverley I suppose so.
Jo Why on earth would she've done that?
Beverley I don't know. Maybe she just likes to have it there. You know. In case she ever feels she wants to …
Jo Fiona? Phone me?
Beverley She's not as bad as all that, you know.
Jo You don't know her!
Beverley Yes, I do.
Jo Oh, yes! So you do.
Beverley Actually, I think she's rather nice.
Jo (*sarcastically*) Evidently!
Beverley So. Why don't you go and find her now, eh? Like I said, she was a bit upset when she ran off. Might be a good opportunity. For a bit of a reconciliation.

Act I   29

Jo Oh no! I'd need to think about it a lot more than that before I start building any bridges.
Beverley Well, I wouldn't think too much. If I were you.
Jo And besides, I'm not running the risk of bumping into your psychopathic brother again.
Beverley Vyvian?
Jo Though it's starting to look as if you're not much better than he is!
Beverley Oh, I'm not as bad as him. Not anything like! I only mow the lawn on Sundays!
Jo Anyone who can go through someone else's handbag is quite capable of forgetting to phone an actress's agent. So I'll have the money now, if you don't mind?
Beverley But I thought you said ——
Jo I'll make an exception — just this once — and negotiate it myself.
Beverley How much do you want?
Jo How much are you offering?
Beverley Fifty quid?
Jo A hundred.
Beverley Seventy-five.
Jo Done. Have you got the cash on you?
Beverley (*feeling for his wallet*) I should have. (*After a lot of searching*) Damn!
Jo What?
Beverley I've lost my wallet.
Jo Very convenient!
Beverley I had it on me when I got here. I paid the taxi driver with a tenner. It must've dropped out when I went to the loo just now. Hang on. (*He heads towards the wings*) I'll go and look.
Jo Don't be too long!
Beverley Don't worry. The loo's only just up one flight of stairs.

Beverley exits

Jo (*with some urgency, calling after him*) Don't be too long!

Jo stands nervously on her own for a moment, then she starts gently to whistle to keep her spirits up, but the whistle fades away into nervous silence

Vyvian pokes his head round the curtain and watches Jo for a few moments with obvious wicked pleasure

Jo doesn't notice Vyvian. He moves up behind her

Vyvian (*quietly, right into Jo's ear*) Hallo, Fiona!

Jo (*jumping away from Vyvian*) Aaagh! (*She turns and sees him*) Oh my God! Red hankie. Vyvian!
Vyvian A pleasure to see you again, Fiona! Or should I say "Jo"!
Jo (*a little cry*) Ah! (*Innocently*) Jo?
Vyvian Jo!
Jo (*in a mock cockney accent, chewing*) I don't know any Jo. (*She continues to pretend to chew during the following*)
Vyvian Oh don't you!
Jo No!
Vyvian You don't know your own sister Jo?
Jo My own sister Jo?
Vyvian You told me all about her just now.
Jo Did I?
Vyvian Or, at any rate, *Fiona* did.
Jo Oh, yeah! That's right. I did.
Vyvian (*fiercely*) You're not Fiona.
Jo (*a little cry*) Oh!
Vyvian And if you don't come clean with me, I'll show you what I do on Sunday!
Jo (*all in a rush, in her own accent*) I'm Jo!
Vyvian That's better! I hate dishonesty. I think you've been playing a little game with me, haven't you? A naughty little game.
Jo (*in a little voice*) Have I?
Vyvian You and my feeble brother Beverley.
Jo You've got a feeble brother Beverley, have you?
Vyvian You don't know him as Bob as well, do you?
Jo (*trying to be flippant*) Bob. Beverley. He's all the same to me.
Vyvian Yes. Feeble! How did he get you here?
Jo What? Here?
Vyvian Yes. What pathetic scheme did he dream up?
Jo I'm supposed to be auditioning.
Vyvian Auditioning?
Jo For you.
Vyvian Oh, for me!
Jo "Keep Your Hands to Yourself."
Vyvian I never touched you!
Jo No, I know.
Vyvian (*darkly*) Not yet, anyway!
Jo That's the name of the play.
Vyvian What play?
Jo The play I was supposed to be auditioning for. I'm really an actress, you see.
Vyvian Are you indeed! Well ... Go on, then.

Act I   31

Jo What?
Vyvian I seem to have little time on my hands. As no-one's turned up for my meeting.
Jo Ah. Yes. He put them all off.
Vyvian Who did?
Jo Beverley. He texted them all.
Vyvian Very enterprising.
Jo So he could have you all to himself.
Vyvian Not had the courage to face me yet, though, has he?
Jo I think he was rather hoping I'd do it for him.
Vyvian He's a feeble man.
Jo With a weak bladder.
Vyvian So — come on!
Jo Come on what?
Vyvian You're an actress. I'm a director. Let's see you audition.
Jo Oh. Right.
Vyvian You never know. This could be your big break.
Jo (*more hopefully*) Oh! Right!
Vyvian I've got a lot of — (*picking his words carefully*) exciting parts in the pipeline that you could play for me.
Jo (*unsure again*) Oh. Right.
Vyvian What are you going to do for me?
Jo Well, I know it was only a small part ...
Vyvian Was it?
Jo For the maid in "Keep Your Hands to Yourself" ...
Vyvian Ah.
Jo But I got hold of a script anyway ...
Vyvian Oh, it actually exists, does it?
Jo Yes. So, I thought I'd do a little bit of Scene 2 — if that's all right?
Vyvian Fire ahead.
Jo I actually have to play three characters in this little bit ...
Vyvian Three!
Jo Just so it all makes sense.
Vyvian Right.
Jo So I hope it won't be too confusing.
Vyvian (*after a moment's thought*) I don't think I can be confused by anything any more.
Jo Good. So. (*She "prepares" herself*)
Vyvian (*having waited long enough*) When you're quite ready?
Jo (*collecting herself*) Oh! Yes. Sorry. (*Turning to one side; in a low voice*) Jack! (*Turning to the other side; in a low voice*) John! (*Turning the other way*) It's you! (*Turning the other way*) It's me! (*Turning the other way*) Then who's ... ? (*She looks down, then turns the other way*) Yes!

Who's ... ? (*She looks down, then crouches and looks up to the front, glancing to both sides. In a squeaky, northern accent*) Hallo. (*She jumps up and turns to one side; in a low voice*) Row-e ——! (*But she interrupts herself, turning to the other side, trying to make it sound as if both Jack and John are speaking at the same time; in a low voice*) Rowena! (*She pauses for a moment, slightly giddy; then, turning to one side, in a low voice*) What are you doing down there? (*Turning to the other side*) Yes! What? (*Crouching on the floor; in the squeaky northern accent*) Well, it is my room, you know. My maid's room. At the top of the house. (*She stands up and turns to one side; in a low voice*) Oh yes, so it is! (*Turning the other way*) So it is! (*Looking up*) What are you doing here, Jack? (*Turning to the other side*) I came to see Rowena. What are you doing here, John? (*Turning to the other side*) Same reason. I didn't see you here when I came in. (*Turning to the other side*) Well, I didn't see you here when I came in! (*Crouching on the floor; squeaky northern voice*) I didn't see *either* of you when *I* came in. The lights were out, weren't they? Only the moon shining in through the casement window. (*She stands up and turns to one side; in a low voice*) So romantic! (*Turning to the other side*) So — enticing! (*Crouching on the floor and getting up; squeaky northern voice*) I didn't bother to put the light on, because I was going to get straight into bed. (*Turning to the other side*) Ooh! (*Turning the other side*) Ooh! (*Facing the front again, squeaky northern voice*) I took me blouse off and dropped it on the floor down here. (*She indicates to one side of her*) Then I took my skirt off and dropped that on the floor down here. (*She indicates to the other side of her*) I bent over to pick up me blouse (*she bends over to one side*) and something touched me here. (*She points to her bottom, then straightens up and turns to one side; in a low voice*) That was me! (*She faces the front again; squeaky northern voice*) I bent over to pick up me skirt (*she bends over to the other side*) and something touched me here. (*She points to her bottom, then straightens up and turns to the other side, in a low voice*) That was me! (*Bending over again; squeaky northern voice*) I stood up — (*she does, then turns to one side; in a low voice*) and something touched me here. (*She points to her crotch, then faces front; squeaky northern voice*) That wasn't me! (*Turning to face the other way; in a low voice*) That was me! (*Turning to the other side*) You? (*Turning to the other side*) yes. Me! (*Turning to the other side*) You bounder! (*She goes to hit the other man, then swaps sides to be the man who's just been hit and manages to actually hit herself on the head. She stands there, swaying*)

Vyvian Hell's bells! Are you all right?
Jo (*still swaying*) Yes. Yes. Fine, thank you! What do you think?
Vyvian (*lost for words*) What do I think?
Jo Could you find anything for me?
Vyvian (*after several attempts; finally*) Yes. Yes, I think I could.
Jo (*getting herself together*) Oh! Great!

Act I 33

Vyvian But it wouldn't be ...
Jo Wouldn't be what?
Vyvian It wouldn't be — (*he searches for the right word*) conventional.
Jo Really?
Vyvian And it would probably have to take place ...
Jo Yes?
Vyvian It would probably have to take place ——
Jo Yes?
Vyvian — on a *Sunday!*
Jo Agh!
Beverley (*voice-over; shouting, angrily*) Vyvian! Vyvian! Where are you?
Vyvian (*to Jo*) Ah. At last! My feeble brother, Beverley. (*Shouting out*) I'm out here, you wimp!
Beverley (*voice-over; shouting, evidently just behind the curtain now*) And I'm just behind here, you bastard! I've been looking for you everywhere!
Vyvian Well, at last you've found me!
Beverley (*voice-over; as before*) I won't let you do it to me!
Vyvian (*shouting out*) Do what?
Beverley (*voice-over; as before*) Ruin my relationship with Cheryl!
Vyvian (*shouting out*) I rather think you've done that for yourself, haven't you?
Beverley (*voice-over; as before*) Come behind here and let me hit you!
Vyvian (*shouting out*) No fear! Why don't you come out here?
Beverley (*after a slight pause; voice-over, as before*) Well, I can't really do that, can I?
Jo (*backing away slightly to the edge of the curtain*) I think he may have a point, you know!
Vyvian (*going up to Jo; angrily*) Do you seriously think I'm going to go round there and let that ——

Vyvian is suddenly yanked behind the curtain by an unseen hand

Agh!

A violent fight ensues behind the curtain. We see hints of it as hands and feet brush against the back of the curtain and we hear shouts and expletives from both Beverley and Vyvian — including Beverley shouting: "A knife! Oh my God, Vyvian!" — as the fight gradually becomes more and more heated

Jo backs away from the fight DS

It all comes to an end in a final scream from Beverley, and his legs (or, rather, those of a double or dummy) flop out on to the floor from behind the curtains. There are a few moments of silence

Vyvian (behaving so that we believe he is Beverley) comes out from behind the curtain, stepping over the legs. He moves down to Jo

(*All of a fluster*) I didn't mean to do it!
Jo Oh my God!
Vyvian I was just trying to fight him off!
Jo What've you *done?*
Vyvian He pulled a knife on me.
Jo Beverley!
Vyvian I think I've killed him.
Jo This is awful.
Vyvian What shall we do?
Jo Just calm down a bit.
Vyvian Calm down a bit? I've just killed my brother!
Jo He may not actually be dead. We'll get an ambulance.
Vyvian (*bursting into tears*) Oh, Vyvian!
Jo Oh — blow your nose, for heaven's sake! You've got snot everywhere.
Vyvian (*still crying*) All right. (*He takes his red handkerchief from his pocket and starts to blow his nose*)
Jo (*seeing Vyvian's handkerchief and stopping dead in her tracks*) Oh my God!
Vyvian (*suddenly not crying any more, but looking at Jo with an evil glint in his eye*) Oh dear. Bad luck, Jo Smith. The wrong brother got it. (*He grabs hold of Jo from behind*)

Jo lets out a little cry

I think it's time to perform a little black mass!
Jo (*hardly able to speak*) On a Friday?

Vyvian produces a knife and puts it to Jo's neck

Vyvian (*grinning*) And you can have the starring role!

Black-out

ACT II

The same. Later

A closed theatrical skip stands just off centre in front of the theatre curtains. Jo is inside it. Beverley's legs still protrude from behind the curtains

The stage is in darkness

Vyvian suddenly pokes his head through a gap in the middle of the curtains, with a grotesque devil half-mask on his face. A tight spot snaps up on him, together with spooky uplighting all over the curtains as if from footlights

Vyvian Ta-ra! It's showtime! (*He moves through the curtain*)

During the next ten seconds or so the Lights return to their Act I state

    What could be better! A darkened theatre! A high priest of the devil! And a helpless young maiden, ripe for sacrifice!
Jo (*voice-over; from the skip*) Help! Let me out of here!
Vyvian (*talking to the skip*) All in good time, my dear! All in good time! First ... I need to prepare! I want everything to be perfect! (*He moves strangely about the stage, humming to himself*)

There is a pause as Vyvian moves about and hums

Jo (*voice-over; from the skip*) What are you doing out there?
Vyvian (*still moving strangely*) I'm summoning up the forces of evil! And banishing the forces of good! Now do be quiet! I need to concentrate.
Jo (*voice-over; from the skip*) Sorry!

Vyvian resumes his humming, still moving strangely about the stage. There is a pause as he does so. He continues to move about in this way during the following

    (*Voice-over; from the skip*) Um — excuse me.
Vyvian (*irritably*) What is it now?
Jo (*voice-over; from the skip*) Wouldn't it be better to leave all this till Sunday?

Vyvian Sunday? Why Sunday?
Jo (*voice-over; from the skip*) Isn't that when you usually do this sort of thing?
Vyvian (*stopping moving to consider this seriously*) Leave it for a full meeting of the society, you mean?
Jo (*voice-over; from the skip*) Yes! Exactly!
Vyvian (*thoughtfully*) Hmm. We'd be able to do things a little more lavishly, I suppose. Acolytes. Attendant priests.
Jo (*voice-over; from the skip*) Sounds lovely.
Vyvian But, on the whole, I think — better not!
Jo (*voice-over; from the skip; a little cry*) Oh!
Vyvian Strike while the iron's hot! Don't you think so? (*He moves strangely about the stage and hums again*)
Jo (*voice-over; from the skip*) But won't your fellow members feel a bit left out?
Vyvian (*still moving strangely*) In what way "left out"?
Jo (*voice-over; from the skip*) Well — if you go ahead and have such a nice time without them all?
Vyvian (*stopping moving to consider*) Oh, I don't know ... (*Explaining*) To be honest with you — we're much more of a "talking and reading about" society than an "actually *doing*" society. The rest of them might find all this hands-on stuff a little bit shocking. (*He moves about strangely again*)
Jo (*voice-over; from the skip*) I'm siding with them!
Vyvian (*suddenly stopping moving; decisively*) Right! There we are! Everything's ready! (*He moves swiftly to the skip and flings the lid open*) Out you come, my dear!
Jo (*standing up in the skip, then catching sight of Vyvian's face*) Oh my God! What on earth have you got on your face?
Vyvian Nothing on earth, my dear. That's the whole point!
Jo It's horrible!
Vyvian Thank you. Now get a move on! We haven't got much time.
Jo (*climbing slowly out of the skip; with false nonchalance*) Oh, I don't see any real need to hurry.
Vyvian Your sobbing sister could be letting herself out of that toilet any time now!
Jo (*surprised*) Fiona's in the loo?
Vyvian She locked herself in there ages ago. She's bawling her eyes out.
Jo (*struck by this thought*) Oh! (*Even a little moved*) Poor old thing.
Vyvian Now stand there and don't move while I get this thing round here. (*He pushes the skip towards the exit round behind the curtain*)
Jo (*just before Vyvian disappears*) Um ... Excuse me.

Vyvian stops in his tracks and looks at Jo for a split second

Act II   37

Vyvian (*sharply*) Yes?
Jo Well ... Don't you want to tie me up or something?
Vyvian (*not believing he's heard what she's said*) What?
Jo I said, "Don't you want to tie me up or something?"
Vyvian Tie you up?
Jo Yes.
Vyvian Me?
Jo In case I make a run for it.
Vyvian (*drawing up to his full height*) I may worship the devil, but I'm not into anything like *that!*
Jo (*giving him a look*) Oh. Right.
Vyvian Besides — (*menacingly*) I've still got my knife!
Jo Oh, yes. So you have.
Vyvian (*moving towards Jo*) If I've killed once, I can kill again.
Jo I thought that's what you were going to do anyway.
Vyvian What?
Jo Kill me.
Vyvian Well, yes! Yes, I am!
Jo So it might just be worth the risk.
Vyvian (*ominously*) I'm not so sure.
Jo (*a little cowed*) No?
Vyvian There are all sorts of different ways of being killed, you know.
Jo (*in a small voice*) Are there?
Vyvian (*warming to his theme*) Oh, yes! For instance, if — while I'm out of sight behind that curtain — I hear even the tiniest hint of a little move from you — then out I shall leap — ferociously — and, like Jack the Ripper, hack your body excruciatingly into a thousand jagged pieces, my face a grotesque tangle of pent-up fury.
Jo Oh yes?
Vyvian Whereas if we leave it until the sacrifice, it'll be one — clean — stroke ... (*an afterthought*) and I might even smile while I'm doing it. (*He demonstrates the smile*)
Jo (*having considered the smile*) No, you're all right.
Vyvian So stay where you are! And not a move! (*He returns to the skip*) I warn you, I have the ears of a bat!
Jo (*out front*) And the legs of an ostrich.
Vyvian (*sharply*) What's that?
Jo (*cheerfully*) Nothing.
Vyvian Now stay still and shut up!

Vyvian pushes the skip off behind the curtain

A few moments later the legs disappear behind the curtain as if Vyvian has dragged them off. We hear Vyvian grunting with effort behind the curtain

Jo makes up her mind to make a move. She eases herself carefully over to the other side of the stage, nearer the exit

Vyvian emerges from behind the curtain pushing the skip. It is now closed

Jo stops dead still

Vyvian pushes the skip c, immediately in front of the curtain. He looks up to where Jo had been, sees she's not there and looks to where she is

You moved!
Jo I know!
Vyvian I said not to!
Jo I'm sorry!
Vyvian Sit down!
Jo Right!
Vyvian Here! (*He indicates the skip*)
Jo Right!
Vyvian And this time — stay still!
Jo I will! (*She sits on the skip, and then suddenly realizes*) Oh my God! Is Beverley inside here? (*She makes to get up again*)
Vyvian (*putting his hands on Jo's shoulders from behind to keep her sitting*) I said, "Stay still!" I want to keep the two of you together.
Jo (*having thought about it*) This is a nightmare!
Vyvian Yes. It is rather fun, isn't it!
Jo Poor Beverley!
Vyvian I didn't actually mean to kill him, you know.
Jo Didn't you?
Vyvian Oh, no. Not at first. I just wanted to give him a bit of a jolt.
Jo Well, you've certainly done that!
Vyvian Oh, no ... No ... Him ending up dead was just a happy accident.
Jo (*outraged*) Happy!
Vyvian Delirious!
Jo How can you say, "happy"?
Vyvian Well, I just open my mouth and ——
Jo (*interrupting Vyvian*) How can Beverley being dead be happy?
Vyvian It's joyous ——
Jo God!
Vyvian — from the point of view of me ending up with Cheryl.
Jo You're unbelievable!
Vyvian Though it's sad, too, of course ——
Jo Oh yes?
Vyvian — from the point of view of his actually being my brother.

Act II

A noise like a raspberry comes from the skip

Vyvian (*noting the noise but ignoring it*) At last! This is it!
Jo Is it?
Vyvian This is the moment I've been waiting for all my life!

Another raspberry comes from the skip

(*Noting the noise again, but going on and getting quite worked up*) Now — finally — I shall be united with my master the devil in one glorious gesture of evil!

A slightly more prolonged raspberry comes from the skip

(*Irritably prosaic; his flow broken*) Look, do you mind!
Jo Mind what?
Vyvian Not — making that noise — while I'm working myself up!
Jo Making what noise?
Vyvian That — (*he makes a raspberry noise*) noise.
Jo Oh, that! No — that's not me. No. That seems to be coming from inside here. (*She indicates the skip she's sitting on*)
Vyvian (*with increasing agitation*) Inside there?
Jo Yes.

They realize simultaneously the implication of what Jo has said and jump away from the skip with a scream. They both stand a little way away on either side of it for a few moments, staring at it

(*At length, in a forced whisper*) It must be Beverley.
Vyvian (*also in a forced whisper*) Beverley?
Jo Who else?
Vyvian But Beverley's dead!
Jo I know!

Another raspberry comes from the skip. Jo and Vyvian both give a little scream

(*After another little pause*) I think I have heard of it before.
Vyvian Heard of what?
Jo Well — you know — corpses — exhaling excess wind — after they've been — well — made into corpses.
Vyvian I've never heard of it before.
Jo Haven't you?

Vyvian Never in my life!
Jo I'm surprised.
Vyvian Are you?
Jo What with all your experience.
Vyvian All of what experience?
Jo Of dead bodies.
Vyvian (*shocked*) What dead bodies?
Jo All the people you've sacrificed.
Vyvian I haven't sacrificed anyone.
Jo (*surprised*) Haven't you?
Vyvian Oh, no! Not me!
Jo I thought you were doing it all the time!
Vyvian (*flustered*) Am I?
Jo Left, right and centre!
Vyvian What about up and down?
Jo And especially on Sundays.
Vyvian But it's only a Friday!
Jo (*a little affronted*) Do you mean to tell me that I'm your first?
Vyvian Well — in a manner of speaking — and — to be absolutely truthful with you — yes!
Jo (*exploding*) Well, if you've never done it before, why on earth are you starting now?
Vyvian (*exploding back*) I don't know! It must be the thrill of actually killing Beverley. It's got me all excited.

Another raspberry comes from the skip

Jo Well, it looks like Beverley's coming back from the dead to have a word with you about it!
Vyvian Bloody hell! I can't stand this! It must be his spirit coming back to torment me!
Jo It could be, I suppose.
Vyvian (*a little scream*) Agh!
Jo Or, on the other hand, it could just be that he wasn't actually dead in the first place.
Vyvian Not dead?
Jo Just out cold.
Vyvian How "out cold"?
Jo In a daze.
Vyvian He wasn't "in a daze"! He was dead! I've never seen anyone more dead in my whole life!
Jo Excuse me, but your experience of dead bodies seems to be growing flimsier by the minute!

Act II

Vyvian Don't be petty! I know a dead body when I see one! I stuck that knife in him right up to the hilt!
Jo Don't you think we should just open it up and have a brief look anyway. Just in case he's still alive?
Vyvian No fear! That's his spirit all right! I haven't been a member of the Wokingham (*or local town*) and District Sons of Satan Society for fifteen years without getting to know a bit about it! Quick! Sit on the skip to stop it coming out!
Jo If it's Beverley's *spirit* farting inside that skip, my sitting on top of it's not going to make much difference!
Vyvian (*frantically*) Well, it can't do any harm, can it! Now sit on the skip and don't argue!
Jo (*sitting on the skip*) All right, all right! Keep your mask on!
Vyvian Ooh, no! My stomach's gone all funny now!

Another raspberry comes from the skip

Jo It seems to run in the family.
Vyvian I think we'll postpone the sacrifice for the moment, if you don't mind.
Jo Oh! And I was so looking forward to it!
Vyvian Perhaps you'll be free sometime next week?
Jo I'll have to check my diary.

Another raspberry comes from the skip, and this time Jo is jolted by someone trying to push the lid up as well

Vyvian I must go to the toilet.
Jo Ooh! Off you go, then!
Vyvian Sorry to rush.

Vyvian rushes off

Jo Don't mind me. (*Calling after him*) Go in the one next to Fiona! You can cheer each other up!

There are another raspberry and jolt from inside the skip

(*Talking to the skip*) Ow! Mind my bum!

Another raspberry and another jolt from inside the skip

OK! OK! Give me a chance to stand up! (*She gets off the skip and stands looking at it*) All clear, then! Out you come!

There is a pause. Nothing happens

I said, "All clear, then! Out you come!"

There is another pause. Then the lid of the skip lifts slightly and Beverley peers out

(*With just a hint of nervousness*) Go on! Put me out of my misery. Are you a ghost?
Beverley Has he gone?
Jo (*with just a hint of panic*) I said, "Put me out of my misery. Are you a ghost?"
Beverley Do I look like a ghost?
Jo How should I know! I've never met one!
Beverley (*irritably*) Of course I'm not a ghost! Has he gone?
Jo Vyvian?
Beverley Yes!
Jo Yes!
Beverley (*standing up in the skip*) Can you believe my brother!
Jo About as much as I can believe you, I think? Why aren't you dead?
Beverley Well — thanks a lot! It's nice to see you alive, as well!
Jo But Vyvian said he stuck his knife into you right up to the hilt.
Beverley Did he hell! He just thought he did!
Jo He seemed pretty convinced about it.
Beverley No. He hit my pocket. So he had to go through several packets of condoms first.
Jo (*after a split second's thought*) I hardly dare ask.
Beverley I carry around a few spares — in case the girls run out. Some protection they offered! I got a really nasty scratch!
Jo And a bit of a scratch made you black out?
Beverley Oh, no! Of course it didn't. No. I realized how excited Vyv was at the idea of killing me, so I thought I'd just play dead for a while. I wanted to see what he was actually going to do.
Jo (*sarcastically*) Oh, fantastic! In the meantime leaving me in the clutches of a supposed devil worshipper!
Beverley I came to your rescue, didn't I? Before he tried anything serious.
Jo By blowing raspberries inside the skip. Brilliant!
Beverley I couldn't think what other noise to make.
Jo They were raspberries, weren't they?
Beverley (*sucking through his teeth; mock seriously*) Takes it out of you, being stabbed to death.
Jo Remind me of that — if I ever think of climbing back inside again.
Beverley Oh! Lord!

Act II

Jo What's the matter?
Beverley How in heaven's name am I going to stop him giving the game away to Cheryl about me and Fiona?
Jo Well, he's not going to give any game away now, is he?
Beverley Isn't he?
Jo No, of course not. Not now he thinks you're dead.
Beverley (*brightening up*) Oh, no. Perhaps you're right.
Jo So that's it, then. Problem solved.
Beverley (*a sudden thought*) Oh, bugger!
Jo What is it now?
Beverley Well ... If Viv's convinced I'm dead ——
Jo Which he is.
Beverley —— then never mind whether he gives anything away about me and Fiona ——
Jo No?
Beverley —— because he's going to think the way's all clear for him to go ahead and get off with Cheryl, anyway!
Jo Oh. Yes. I didn't think about that.
Beverley So sooner or later he's going to have to find out that I'm still alive.
Jo If you want to be in with a chance, yes.
Beverley Yes. And the moment he does, we're right back to square one! He'll tell her all about me and Fiona.
Jo *You're* right back to square one, you mean. Don't get me involved in any of this. I'm only doing a job.
Beverley Oh. Right. So you are.
Jo For which I haven't yet been paid.
Beverley Ah. No. Sorry. I found my wallet. (*Getting his wallet out and opening it up*) Seventy-five, did we say?
Jo Seventy-five.
Beverley (*counting it out*) Here you are. (*He holds the money out to Jo*)
Jo (*taking hold of it*) Thanks.
Beverley (*suddenly having a brainwave and not letting go of it*) Unless ...
Jo (*having waited a moment*) Unless what?
Beverley I don't suppose — if I made it a hundred — you'd help me a bit more, would you?
Jo Help you how?
Beverley Well — it's just occurred to me, you see ... (*He pauses while he works it out*)
Jo (*after a moment*) Yes?
Beverley It's just occurred to me — that if I can convince Vyvian I've actually been over to the other side ...
Jo (*looking behind her*) What other side?
Beverley No. The *other* side!

Jo (*looking the other way*) What? Over there?
Beverley No. Not any other side here! To Hell, I mean!
Jo Oh. *That* other side.
Beverley Yes! If I can convince him that I've actually met the devil — and that the devil's sent me back and given me another chance — then Vyvian'll be so impressed he won't dare to try and interfere between me and Cheryl.
Jo How on earth are you going to persuade Vyvian of all that?
Beverley Well — he's half-way there already, isn't he? He's so into all this black magic nonsense, he'll probably leap at it. All we need to do is to dress it up a bit.
Jo (*suspiciously*) In what way "dress it up"?
Beverley Well, this is a theatre, isn't it? Surely they must have some kind of sound system here? Where I can amplify my voice. Bend it a bit, maybe. (*Getting excited*) Perhaps I could even use some lights, as well. Organize a flash of lightning, or something. Ooh! This is really exciting! I can't wait to see the look on his face!
Jo Hold on a minute, Trevor Nunn! Before you get too carried away, where do I fit into all of this?
Beverley Well, it'll take a bit of setting up. I'll need someone to keep him out of the way until I'm ready.
Jo Have you ever worked the sound and lights in a theatre before?
Beverley No, I can't say I have, not really, no.
Jo Well, that's going to be great, then, isn't it!
Beverley I can figure them out! But it'll take a few moments. That's why I need you to keep him busy for a while.
Jo Well — to tell you the truth — I think I'll leave it at the seventy-five.
Beverley I'll make it a hundred and twenty.
Jo No. You're all right. It's not just the money. I'm not totally mercenary, you know.
Beverley What is it, then?
Jo Well ...
Beverley You're not still afraid of Vyvian, are you?
Jo Oh, God, no! No. Vyvian's just a pussycat — with rather sharp claws.
Beverley What, then?
Jo No. I think — when it comes down to it — the problem — actually — is you.
Beverley Me!
Jo That's right.
Beverley What in heaven's name have *I* done?
Jo Well, I'm just wondering — as you reveal to me more and more of your wonderful talent for deception — whether, after all, Charlotte might not be better off with Vyvian.

Act II

Beverley Charlotte might be, but Cheryl certainly wouldn't!
Jo That's who I meant.
Beverley I know you did! What d'you mean, she'd be better off with Vyvian! He's a low down, murdering devil-worshipper!
Jo He hasn't actually murdered anyone, as far as I can see.
Beverley It wasn't for want of trying, was it!
Jo I'm only saying how it looks ——
Beverley But we're engaged!
Jo — to a disinterested outsider.
Beverley I love her!
Jo That didn't seem to count for much when you were having your little bit of fun with Fiona, did it?
Beverley I've told you! That was just a lapse! A silly mistake!
Jo Well, your silly mistake is sobbing her heart out in the loo ——
Beverley I know. I'm sorry.
Jo — next to the brother you've just scared witless by farting in that skip.
Beverley Besides — I've bought her a present.
Jo Who? Fiona?
Beverley No. Cheryl, of course. I've bought her a sorry present.
Jo Oh! Cheap, was it?
Beverley No! Not a sorry present. A present to show I'm sorry!
Jo Oh. But I thought the idea was she wouldn't end up knowing you've got anything to be sorry about!
Beverley No! I know! But I must do *something* to salve my conscience. She'll think I'm giving it to her because I'm glad to see her after all this time — and I am, of course — of course I am! — but I'll know secretly to myself that I'm giving it to her to say "I'm sorry."
Jo I think I follow that.
Beverley Here — look ... (*He gets a jewellery box out of his pocket*) Here it is. Have a look for yourself. (*He hands the box to Jo*) It was really expensive! Surely that'll show you how sorry I am.
Jo (*opening the box and taking out a necklace; impressed*) Oh!
Beverley It's a necklace.
Jo I can see that. It's beautiful.
Beverley I know. (*Poetically*) Just like Cheryl.
Jo All right. You've convinced me.
Beverley Thank heavens for that!
Jo Two hundred pounds.
Beverley Well — no — not quite as much as that, actually.
Jo No. I'm negotiating again.
Beverley Oh. Are you?
Jo Two hundred.
Beverley Oh. Yes. I see what you mean. One-forty.

Jo One-eighty.
Beverley One-sixty.
Jo Done!
Beverley There you go, then. (*He counts out some notes from his wallet and hands them to Jo*) Here's a hundred now.
Jo Hang on!
Beverley You can have the rest when the job's done. Fair's fair. Now. Let's get on with it. You're an actress. Where do you think all the sound and lighting stuff'll be kept?
Jo Well, it's usually in the lighting box.
Beverley (*setting off*) Right. I'll go and find it. (*Stopping to check*) By the way, how big is this box?
Jo No. The lighting box isn't a box.
Beverley Isn't it?
Jo No. It's a room.
Beverley Is it?
Jo (*pointing out into the auditorium*) Of course it is. It'll be up at the back, somewhere.
Beverley (*looking where she's pointed*) Up at the back. Jolly good. How do I get to it?
Jo You'll find a door to front of house one side or the other. After that, follow your nose!
Beverley (*heading off*) Right you are. Here I go. (*Muttering to himself as he goes*) I don't know why they can't just call it the lighting *room* if it's a room. Wretched theatricals!

Beverley exits

Jo realizes she is still holding the necklace

Jo (*calling after Beverley*) Oh! Beverley! Wait! The necklace! (*To herself*) Oh. Well. He can have it back later. This is going to be money for old rope. I can't see Vyvian coming out of that loo in a hurry.

Janet enters R. He is a man identical to Beverley and Vyvian though wearing a raincoat

Jo turns and sees him. She studies him for a long time

Where's your hankie?
Janet (*real cockney accent*) My 'ankie?
Jo No hankie. Right! Good. He is still in the loo. I thought he would be. You don't need a coat on, you know. The lighting box won't be outside.

Act II   47

Janet Lighting box?
Jo It'll be up at the back somewhere. Like I just said.
Janet I don't think so.
Jo No. It will be.
Janet You didn't say anything to me.
Jo Yes, I did.
Janet Not as I recall.
Jo (*after studying him again for a second more. With growing horror*) Oh my God! You're not another one, are you?
Janet If — by some strange and unnatural coincidence much favoured by comic playwrights from the third century BC Greeks onwards — but I digress — if — by some such chance — you've 'appened to meet both of my two identical elder brothers — then, "Yes! I'm another one!"
Jo Bloody hell!
Janet Language!
Jo You're Beverley and Vyvian's identical younger brother?
Janet That is the case.
Jo Bloody hell!
Janet 'Ere! I've just warned you.
Jo And are you in the theatre, as well?
Janet (*looking around him*) Well, yes, I think so.
Jo No. I don't mean that! I mean are you involved in the theatre?
Janet Oh, I see. Yes. That's very astute of you, young lady.
Jo Not really. All that talk of comic playwrights.
Janet I am indeed a treader of the boards ——
Jo I thought so.
Janet — though only in my spare time.
Jo Oh, yes?
Janet I'm a paid up life member of the Crowthorne (*or local town*) Amateur Shakespeare Players.
Jo Are you really?
Janet You should've seen my Bottom. It was much talked of in Ascot. (*Or local town*)
Jo I'm sure it was.
Janet Must run in the blood, I suppose. What with Vyvian, an' all. Though I 'aven't in'erited any of 'is darker side — I'm glad to say.
Jo So what do you do for a living? Are you a charity worker as well?
Janet In a manner of speaking, yes. I am.
Jo What are you?
Janet I'm a copper.
Jo Golly! Are you?
Janet In the Vice Squad.
Jo God!

Janet Detective Inspector Janet Jones, at your service.
Jo (*about to say something else, and then realizing*) Janet?
Janet Our mother gave up all pretence by the time I came along.
Jo That must've been hell at school.
Janet It wasn't good, I grant you.
Jo Did you never think of changing it?
Janet Again, very astute of you. It did cross my mind, yes. But it comes in very 'andy, you know. In my line of business.
Jo Does it?
Janet Undercover work. Invaluable. Throws people off the scent, you see. Being called Janet.
Jo (*sure she's dealing with a lunatic*) Right. Good. So, you've come here to see Vyvian, have you?
Janet Oh! 'E's 'ere, is 'e?
Jo Yes. He's upstairs. In the loo.
Janet I see!
Jo Or is it Beverley you want?
Janet Beverley?
Jo He's knocking about here somewhere too.
Janet Quite a family party!
Jo Do the three of you often get together in the same place?
Janet (*with a wry look*) Not if we can 'elp it, no.
Jo No, I see what you mean.
Janet What's 'e doing 'ere, then?
Jo Beverley?
Janet 'Oo else?
Jo He's come to see Vyvian.
Janet I didn't think the two of them was talking ——
Jo I'm not so sure they are!
Janet — what with all this Cherie business.
Jo Charlotte … (*Correcting herself*) Cheryl!
Janet That's the one.
Jo Now you're here, perhaps you could act as a go-between.
Janet Oh, no, no, no, no, no! I 'aven't got time for any of this long-drawn-out family business!
Jo Haven't you?
Janet I'm 'ere in an official capacity, as an officer of the Vice Squad, to 'ave a little word with a particular young lady.
Jo Oh, yes?
Janet A particular young lady of a certain not-so-very-honourable profession.
Jo (*thinking of Fiona*) Oh! God!
Janet And I 'ave reason to believe ——
Jo Yes?

Act II   49

Janet — from information received ——
Jo Yes?
Janet — that that particular young lady ——
Jo Yes?
Janet — is yourself.
Jo Me!
Janet You fit the description perfectly.
Jo What description?
Janet Given to me at my brother's 'ostel for unfortunates not fifteen minutes ago. (*Getting his notebook out*) Allow me to quote: (*reading*) "Short, cuddly blonde with a roving eye." (*He looks up sharply*) You see my point! You're Fiona Smith and no mistake!
Jo (*trying out the roving eye*) I'm not so sure about the roving eye.
Janet (*impatiently*) That's metaphorical, not physical!
Jo And doesn't "cuddly" just mean fat? Bit of an insult, that.
Janet Not at all! There's no (*anglicizing the phrase*) *double entendre* intended. It means what it says: "cuddly".
Jo Well I'm not Fiona! However accurate your description is!
Janet Well, you are from where I'm standing. You were seen coming in 'ere by the proprietor of the sandwich establishment over the road.
Jo Well that's as maybe, but from where *I'm* standing, I'm Fiona's identical twin sister, Jo.
Janet (*brought up short*) Fiona Smith has an identical twin sister called Jo?
Jo Yes. That's me.
Janet I find that a bit hard to swallow.
Jo You can talk! With all your lot!
Janet Point taken. But you must see my dilemma.
Jo What dilemma?
Janet 'Ow can I be sure you genuinely are Fiona Smith's twin sister Jo, and not just Fiona Smith *pretending* to be 'er twin sister Jo?
Jo Yes. I see what you mean.
Janet Do you have any means of identification on you?
Jo (*thinking*) Identification ...
Janet Driving licence?
Jo I don't drive.
Janet Union card?
Jo Oh, damn! I left my Equity card at home.
Janet (*his ears pricking up*) Equity?
Jo Yes. I'm an actress.
Janet Actress, eh? (*In danger of being star-struck*) Professional?
Jo Absolutely.
Janet (*impressed*) 'Ow exciting! Would I 'ave seen you in anything on the telly?

Jo Well — I had a small part in *The Bill*.
Janet Did you now!
Jo A very small part.
Janet I never watch it.
Jo No?
Janet Too close to 'ome.
Jo Yes, of course. And then I was in a car advert earlier in the year.
Janet A car advert, eh?
Jo But it was only shown during the day.
Janet Ooh, the day's a bad time for me.
Jo Is it?
Janet I'll either be working ——
Jo I see.
Janet — or sleeping.
Jo Right.
Janet Anything else?
Jo No, not really.
Janet Pity, that.
Jo I know.
Janet Could've 'elped with the identification.
Jo (*puzzled*) Could it?
Janet (*brightly*) Still, all is not lost.
Jo No?
Janet You can prove it to me now.
Jo Prove what?
Janet That you're an actress.
Jo Can I? How?
Janet By doing me a little speech. Isn't that what actresses usually do?
Jo Well, yes, but …
Janet (*settling himself down on the skip*) Fire ahead, then. I'm all ears.
Jo (*slowly*) Right. (*Almost to herself*) This is turning into a very weird day. (*To Janet*) Well, I've got this piece from a farce …
Janet (*dubiously*) A farce?
Jo "Keep Your Hands to Yourself."
Janet I'm from the Vice Squad. I can touch what I like.
Jo No. That's the name of the farce.
Janet Oh, no, no, no, no, no, young lady. You can aim 'igher than that.
Jo Can I?
Janet Why not give me a little bit of the Master himself?
Jo Which master is that?
Janet The Bard of Avon.
Jo Shakespeare, you mean.
Janet Surely you, a professional actress, have got a little bit from the canon of thirty-seven up your sleeve that you can trot out for me now?

Act II

Jo Well, yes. Of course I have.
Janet Off you go, then. What are you going to do for me?
Jo Well, I usually do a bit of Oberon from *A Midsummer Night's Dream*.
Janet 'Ang on, 'ang on! Oberon's a man's part!
Jo I know! Why do people always say that? The men's parts are more interesting than the women's. I don't see why they should always have all the fun.
Janet Oh, well. Go ahead if you must — though it seems like a most ill-advised venture if you want my opinion.
Jo OK. I think I can remember it. Here we go. (*She is rather good, making sense of the verse and not getting bogged down in rhyme and rhythm. She creates quite a magical effect*)

> What hast thou done? Thou hast mistaken quite,
> And laid the love juice on some true love's sight.
> Of thy misprision must perforce ensue
> Some true love turned, and not a false turned true.
>
> About the wood go swifter than the wind,
> And Helena of Athens look thou find.
> All fancy-sick she is, and pale of cheer
> With sighs of love, that cost her fresh blood dear.
> By some illusion see thou bring her here.
> I'll charm his eyes against she do appear.
>> Flower of this purple dye,
>> Hit with Cupid's archery,
>> Sink in the apple of his eye.
>> When his love he doth espy,
>> Let her shine as gloriously
>> As the Venus of the sky.
>> When thou wakest, if she be by,
>> Beg of her for remedy.

There is a pause. Jo waits

Janet (*at length, unimpressed*) Is that it?
Jo Yes. What do you think?
Janet Well, I've seen better in Bagshot (*or local town*).
Jo Oh. Have you? Well, I haven't actually had to do that one for a little while.
Janet I think you'd find it a good deal more effective if you took the trouble to observe rhymes in the speech ——
Jo Oh. Really?

Janet — in the way that Steve Wakefield, our Oberon in Crowthorne (*or local town*), was discerning enough so to do. "Wind" and "find" are obvious examples, and I quote: (*he overemphasizes the rhythm and pronounces "find" to rhyme with "wind"*)
>About the wood go swifter than the wind,
>And 'Elena of Athens look thou find

Makes just a little bit more sense of the poetry that way, doesn't it? "Purple dye" and "archery" (*pronounced to rhyme with "dye"*) are two other cases in point.

Jo Yes. Possibly.

Janet 'Owever, I'm not 'ere to give you an acting seminar, am I?

Jo No. You're not.

Janet And you've just about proved your point, I suppose — given that Shakespeare's not your speciality.

Jo (*cheerfully*) Oh. Thanks! (*Having realized what he's just said*) I think.

Janet Where is she, then?

Jo Who?

Janet Your twin sister. Fiona Smith. The young lady of a certain not-so-very-honourable profession. My informant assured me she was coming 'ere. Not often wrong, my informant.

Jo Well ...

Janet Is she 'ere?

Jo Er ...

Janet 'Ave you seen 'er?

Jo Well ...

Janet I assume she was coming 'ere to see you.

Jo Oh, no. She didn't know *I'd* be here.

Janet Aha! So you 'ave seen 'er, then?

Jo Well — not exactly ...

Janet Come on, now. No prevarication. You don't want to be facing a charge of obstruction, now, do you?

Jo No. No, I don't. You see, I haven't actually *seen* her ...

Janet (*suspiciously*) Go on.

Jo But I have *heard* her.

Janet 'Eard 'er?

Jo When she first came in.

Janet (*exasperated*) So where is she now, then?

Jo Well, I'm not exactly sure where she is just at the moment.

Janet Is that so!

Jo Look, why don't you have a little look around for yourself. I'm sure you'll have a better chance of finding her than I will. Professional training and all that.

Janet Well, you could be right. I will 'ave a little shifty. (*He turns to go, then turns back*) You won't be leaving the premises yourself, will you?

Act II 53

Jo (*rather resignedly*) It's looking less and less likely.
Janet Might need to 'ave another little word with you before I go. In the course of my enquiry.
Jo I'll look forward to it.
Janet By the way, why are you 'ere yourself? I don't think we've quite established that yet.
Jo Haven't we?
Janet I don't think so.
Jo I came for an audition — in the first place.
Janet Audition, eh?
Jo Yes.
Janet (*turning to go*) Well, I 'ope it went better than the one you did just now. That was very mediocre.

Janet exits

Jo (*calling after him; indignantly*) It did! Thank you! Why don't you try looking for Fiona under the stage first?
Janet (*off; calling*) Thank you. I will.
Jo (*to herself*) Oh my God. She may be a black sheep but I can't let them arrest her. Mum and Dad would never forgive me! Now then — where's this toilet? I'd better warn her.

Jo hurries off

A loud feedback noise is heard over the speakers

Beverley (*voice-over; from the theatre speakers*) Ah. Good. Found it at last. Heavens, it's tiny! Maybe "box" was right after all! Ah. Here's where they work the lights.

Black-out

Oops!

All the Lights come on again

Where's all the sound stuff? I think it's over here. Agh!

There is the sound of Beverley falling over with a loud crash

Ow! Fancy leaving a box lying about in the middle of a box. How stupid is that! Ah. Here's a microphone. I wonder if it's on.

The thunderous sound of someone tapping a microphone is heard

(*Very loud, as if very close to the mike; in a silly voice*) Halloo! Halloo! (*Away from the mike again*) Oh, Lord! It is on. I'll turn it off. I don't want to give the game away too soon. Where's the switch? Ah.

A loud click is heard as the mike is switched off

Vyvian pokes his head on to the stage. He has the mask pushed up on his head and looks quite shaken. He looks to see who's about and then creeps tentatively up to the skip and after several failed attempts finally screws up enough courage to open the lid and look inside. He finds it empty

Vyvian (*with a sigh of relief*) Oh, thank the devil for that! He's not in there! (*He sits on the skip and takes off the mask to wipe his forehead with the red hankie*) Oh, hell's bells! I can't take much more of this. I've bitten off more than I bargained for! I mean, I've conjured up more than I can chew! Oh, bloody hell! I haven't the faintest idea what I do mean. (*Catching sight of the mask*) That's it! I'm through with you! No more devil worshipping for me! I can't take the consequences. (*He chucks the mask into the skip and wipes his forehead again, then stops suddenly as a new more terrifying thought occurs to him*) Just a minute ... If he's not in *there* — then he must've got out — and be loose in the theatre somewhere — on the look-out for me! (*He hurriedly stuffs the hankie in a side pocket out of sight*) Oh, hell's bells!

Jo hurries on and sees Vyvian

Jo (*urgently*) Ah! There you are!
Vyvian (*turning to see her; with a little scream*) Agh! Here I am.
Jo Haven't you found the box yet?
Vyvian What box?
Jo Never mind about that now. She's coming down here.
Vyvian Is she?
Jo I told her to hide, but she won't listen to me. The moment she saw me she started screaming.
Vyvian Oh dear!
Jo She says she must speak to you.
Vyvian Must she?
Jo It's a matter of life and death.
Vyvian Oh, bloody hell!
Jo Perhaps *you* can get her to hide. Otherwise he'll find her for sure.
Vyvian Who? The spirit?

Act II

Jo No. The policeman.
Vyvian What policeman?
Jo Your brother Janet. From the Vice Squad.
Vyvian Janet's here?
Jo I've just told you, haven't I? He's come here looking for her.
Vyvian He's looking for the actress?
Jo No, no! Not the actress! I'm the actress, you berk! He's looking for the prostitute!
Fiona (*voice-over, calling; emotionally*) Bob! Where are you, Bob?
Jo Here she comes now! I'd better make myself scarce or she'll start screaming again and have Janet up here before you can say Jack Robinson!
Vyvian Is Jack Robinson here as well?
Jo (*hurrying towards the exit*) For God's sake, Beverley! What's the matter with you? Just get her to hide! (*Turning back*) Oh. Here's your necklace back, by the way. (*She gives the necklace to him*)
Vyvian But ...
Jo (*hurrying towards the exit*) I'll come back in a minute and check to see if you've got her out of the way.

Jo exits

Vyvian (*calling after her; ineffectually*) But ... But — I'm not ... I'm not Beverley! Beverley's dead. (*With dread*) Have you communicated with him? Do you know where he is?

Fiona hurries on in a state

Fiona (*rushing up to him*) Bob! Bob! There you are! Bob, I've got to talk to you!
Vyvian No, you haven't!
Fiona (*a serious sing-song version*) Der! Yes I have! We can't just end it like this.
Vyvian I think we might have to ——
Fiona No. I can't bear it!
Vyvian — if you don't hide quickly.
Fiona Hide? Jo wanted me to hide. Why does everyone want me to hide? Am I that ugly?
Vyvian No! You're not ugly at all. It's just that my brother's here.
Fiona What? The one that works in the sandwich shop?
Vyvian No. Not him! Another one.
Fiona You've got another brother?
Vyvian Yes. And this one works for the Vice Squad.
Fiona Vice Squad!

Vyvian He's coming here looking for you.
Fiona Oh, shoot! I must hide!
Vyvian That's what I said.
Fiona Where? Where can I hide?
Vyvian (*looking about him*) Well ...
Fiona (*frantically*) Where can I hide? Quickly!
Vyvian (*reluctantly looking at the skip*) Well — you'd better get in there.
Fiona (*hurrying to the skip*) In here?
Vyvian I think you'll have to.
Fiona (*hurriedly climbing into the skip*) You won't let him find me, will you?
Vyvian Don't worry. I won't let him find you. (*He closes the skip and then gingerly sits on the top of it*)

There is a pause

Fiona (*voice-over, from the skip; plaintively*) Bob?
Vyvian (*after a moment, realizing she means him*) Yes?
Fiona (*voice-over, from the skip*) I love you, Bob.
Vyvian No, you don't.
Fiona (*voice-over, from the skip; in danger of becoming tearful again*) Der! Yes I do.
Vyvian No. Listen. It's not me you love.
Fiona (*voice-over, from the skip; on the edge*) How can you say that?
Vyvian Because I'm not Bob.
Fiona (*voice-over, from the skip; suddenly not tearful*) Yes, you are.
Vyvian No, I'm not. I'm Bob's identical twin brother, Vyvian.
Fiona (*voice-over, from the skip*) Are you?
Vyvian Yes.

There is a pause

Fiona (*voice-over, from the skip*) Are *you* the one that works in the sandwich shop?
Vyvian (*after a brief hesitation; almost kindly*) Yes, that's me.

There is a pause

Fiona (*voice-over, from the skip*) You're not at all how I remember you!

Vyvian fails to think of a reply

Jo appears on stage

Jo (*seeing Vyvian on his own*) Ah.

Act II

Vyvian (*hurriedly shutting her up*) Sh! (*He waves his hands and puts his finger to his lips to stop her*)

Jo cottons on and points to the skip in query. Vyvian answers with a thumbs-up sign

Fiona (*voice-over, from the skip*) Vyvian?
Vyvian Yes?
Jo (*unable to stop herself*) Vyvian!
Vyvian (*to Jo, in a hiss*) Sh!
Jo (*mouthing silently to Vyvian*) Where's your hankie?
Vyvian (*mouthing silently to Jo*) What?
Jo (*mouthing silently to Vyvian, with an elaborate mime*) Your hankie! Where is it!
Vyvian (*mouthing silently to Jo, looking at her as if she's mad, and producing the handkerchief from his pocket*) Here! (*He tucks it back in his breast pocket, leaving it visible*)
Jo (*mouthing silently to herself*) Oh my God! Vyvian! (*Mouthing silently to the back of the auditorium and pointing at Vyvian*) Vyvian!
Vyvian (*out loud to the skip*) Yes, Fiona? What is it?
Fiona (*voice-over, from the skip*) It smells a bit funny in here.
Vyvian Does it?
Fiona (*voice-over, from the skip*) Just a bit, yes.
Vyvian (*scaring himself again*) That'll be the spirit.
Fiona (*voice-over, from the skip*) What spirit?
Vyvian They always leave something of an aura behind them. I've read all about it.
Fiona (*voice-over, from the skip*) Ooh! I feel all creepy. Whose spirit are we talking about?
Vyvian Beverley's.
Fiona (*voice-over, from the skip; puzzled*) Beverley's?
Vyvian I mean Bob's.
Fiona (*voice-over, from the skip; shocked*) Bob's!
Vyvian Yes.
Fiona (*voice-over, from the skip; threatening to wail again*) Are you telling me that Bob's dead?
Vyvian As dead as a doornail. And his spirit's out to get me.

There is a loud squeal over the speakers

Beverley (*voice-over*) Oh, bugger!

The speakers click off

Vyvian (*in a panic*) There he is now!
Fiona (*voice-over, from the skip, horrified*) Ooowww!
Vyvian He's coming to get me!
Fiona (*voice-over, from the skip*) Ooowww!
Jo (*to Vyvian, out loud*) Quick! Go back and hide in that loo!
Vyvian Hide in the toilet?
Jo Yes! You'll be safe in there.
Vyvian What makes you think that?
Jo Well ... Spirits are afraid of water, aren't they?
Vyvian Are they? I don't remember reading anything about that.
Jo It's a well-known fact. Drowns them completely! Now, go on! Hurry up and hide!
Vyvian (*hurrying towards the exit*) I think I need to go back there anyway!

Vyvian exits

Fiona (*voice-over, from the skip, wailing*) Ooowww! Bob's dead!
Jo (*going to the skip*) Oh, do be quiet, Fiona!
Fiona (*voice-over, from the skip; suddenly suspicious*) Who's that speaking out there?
Jo (*knowing what the reaction will be*) It's me. Jo.
Fiona (*voice-over, from the skip; a big scream*) Agh! Go away and leave me alone! You haven't spoken to me for ten years! Why are you starting now?
Jo It was you who walked out on us, you know! We didn't ask you to leave.
Fiona (*voice-over, from the skip*) I can't stand any more of this! I'm coming out!
Jo (*hurriedly holding down the lid of the skip*) No! Don't do that!
Janet (*off; calling*) Well, there's no sign of her under the stage!
Jo (*to the skip, urgently*) Here comes Janet now!
Fiona (*voice-over, from the skip*) Who's Janet?
Jo The Vice Squad officer.
Fiona (*voice-over, from the skip*) I thought she was a bloke!
Jo She is! Now shut up and keep quiet!

Janet enters

Jo sits on the skip

Janet (*to Jo*) Fiona Smith?
Jo I'm afraid not. Still Jo.
Janet I see.
Jo Still not found her?
Janet Not as yet.

Act II 59

Jo Have you tried the flies?
Janet I beg your pardon?
Jo The flies. You know — (*pointing upwards*) up there.
Janet Oh! I see! A professional term! Thanks very much for the advice, miss. I'll waste no time.

Janet exits

There is a brief pause

Fiona (*voice-over, from the skip*) Has he gone?
Jo Yes. But he may come back any minute, so don't move!
Fiona (*voice-over, from the skip, in a wail*) Oooh! My poor Bob! He's dead!
Jo No, Fiona, he's not dead.
Fiona (*voice-over, from the skip*) The man from the sandwich shop said he was.
Jo What man from the sandwich shop?
Fiona (*voice-over, from the skip*) Bob's brother Vyvian.
Jo Vyvian's not from any sandwich shop. He's a famous theatre director. Didn't you talk to each other in that loo just now?
Fiona (*voice-over, from the skip*) Was Vyvian in the loo?
Jo You were in there together for about twenty minutes.
Fiona (*voice-over, from the skip*) Oh, yeah. Someone did come in. But I was too busy thinking about Bob to talk to anyone. And whoever it was seemed quite occupied himself. He had the most terrible runs.
Jo Well — anyway — he's not!
Fiona (*voice-over, from the skip*) Who's not? Not what?
Jo Bob. He's not dead — and he's not Bob, either, come to think of it!
Fiona (*voice-over, from the skip; hopefully*) Bob's not dead after all? Are you sure?
Jo Quite sure. I was talking to him not ten minutes ago.
Fiona (*voice-over, from the skip; joyfully*) But that's wonderful! I must go and find him.

The top of the skip moves as if Fiona is trying to get out

Jo (*sitting firmly on it*) Oh no you don't! Janet's still on the warpath, remember?
Fiona (*voice-over, from the skip*) Oh, yeah. I forgot. I'm so happy about Bob. Hey! What do you mean, "He's not Bob, either"?
Jo His name's Beverley really.
Fiona Beverley?
Jo He calls himself Bob at the hostel so all you girls won't make fun of him.

Fiona (*voice-over, from the skip*) What a sod! You'd think he'd've told his real name to *me!*
Jo And he's engaged as well.
Fiona (*voice-over, from the skip*) I know. (*Starting to cry again*) And he's going back to her an'all. (*She wails*)
Jo (*comfortingly*) Oh. Never mind, Fee. I'd say you were better off without him.

There is another wail from the skip

Why don't you just go home, eh? Hop on a train and go back to Mum and Dad.
Fiona (*voice-over, from the skip*) How can I? I have got a pimp, you know. He'll never let me go without a fight, and I couldn't bring all that back home to Mum and Dad.
Jo Oh — God! I'm sure you and I could sort something out between us.
Beverley (*over the speakers*) Jo? Jo? Hallo, Jo. Is that you down there?
Jo (*gathering herself together and looking up to the back of the auditorium*) Yes. Yes, Beverley. It's me.
Fiona (*voice-over, from the skip*) Is that him? Bob ... Beverley, I mean?
Jo (*in a whisper, to the skip*) Yes. Now keep quiet and listen! This should put you off him forever.
Beverley (*over the speakers, suspiciously*) You are Jo, aren't you? You're not Fiona in disguise?
Jo (*with a wry smile, to the back of the auditorium*) No. No, I'm Jo all right.
Beverley (*over the speakers*) Great! Look, I think I'm ready.
Jo (*to the back of the auditorium, sarcastically*) Oh! Fantastic!
Beverley (*over the speakers*) Is Vyvian about anywhere?
Jo (*to the back of the auditorium*) No, no. He's still shut away safely in the loo.
Beverley (*over the speakers*) Great! Now then, have a listen to this.

There is the most almighty crash of thunder over the speakers, together with a sudden flash of lightning. Jo is shell-shocked. There is a pause

What do you think?
Jo (*to the back of the auditorium*) Beverley, I thought you were trying to give him a fright, not scare him half to death!
Beverley (*over the speakers*) Do you think it's too much?
Jo (*to the back of the auditorium*) The state Vyvian's in at the moment, I think an episode of *Scooby Doo* would be too much!
Beverley (*over the speakers*) Well, it's too late to do anything else now. We'll just have to run with it as it is. Go and bring him down, can you?

Act II 61

Jo (*to the back of the auditorium*) Anything you say, Herr Director! (*To the skip*) You see what I mean? He's barking!
Fiona (*voice-over, from the skip*) He's got a lovely voice, though.
Jo (*to the skip*) You're barking as well!
Beverley (*over the speakers*) Hurry up, Jo! I'm looking forward to this!
Jo (*to the back of the auditorium*) OK! OK! I'm going as fast as I can.
Beverley (*over the speakers*) Oh — by the way — you've still got that necklace, haven't you?
Jo (*to the back of the auditorium*) No, I haven't. I gave it back to you.
Beverley (*over the speakers*) No, you didn't.
Jo (*to the back of the auditorium*) Yes, I did.
Beverley (*over the speakers, panic rising*) No, you didn't.
Jo (*to the back of the auditorium, suddenly thinking*) No, you're right, I didn't. I gave it to Vyvian by mistake.
Beverley (*over the speakers, trying to keep himself under control*) You gave it to Vyvian!
Jo (*to the back of the auditorium*) Yes. Sorry. I thought he was you.
Beverley (*over the speakers*) Oh, for heaven's sake!
Jo (*to the back of the auditorium*) I didn't do it on purpose!
Beverley (*over the speakers*) Oh! Well! It's done now, isn't it! We'll just have to get it back from him later. When he's in shock.

Vyvian enters behind Jo, obviously not scared now at all

Oh, this is going to be brilliant! With that crash of thunder — and the lightning — and then my voice booming out all over the theatre — he'll definitely believe I've met the devil and been sent back to make his life hell! Not just got a bit of a scratch and then pretended to be dead.
Vyvian (*to the back of the auditorium, making Jo jump*) If you want to pull a stunt like that, dearest brother, it's better not to turn on the backstage tannoy and broadcast the whole scheme to the dressing-room speakers! You must've hit the switch by mistake while you were fiddling about up there. I've heard absolutely everything you've just said.
Beverley (*over the speakers*) Oh, heavens!
Vyvian (*to the back of the auditorium*) So it won't be *you* coming back from the dead to get *me* ——
Beverley (*over the speakers, pretending innocence*) Won't it? What do you mean?
Vyvian (*to the back of the auditorium*) — it'll be me coming up there to get you!
Beverley (*over the speakers*) Oh! God!
Vyvian (*to the back of the auditorium*) And I'm on my way now!
Jo Vyvian … ?

Vyvian You keep out of this, my dear. I think you've done quite enough already, don't you?
Jo (*innocently*) Do you?
Vyvian I admire your pluck, though! I like a girl with a bit of spunk in her!
Jo (*strangely warmed by this*) Oh! Thanks!
Beverley (*over the speakers*) Oh. God. The door's jammed shut! I can't get it open from in here.
Vyvian (*to the back of the auditorium*) Don't worry, dearest brother. I'll kick it open from the outside. Here I come now.

Vyvian exits

Beverley (*over the speakers*) Oh, great heavens!
Jo Oh, God! Perhaps I should go after him. He's still got that knife.
Fiona (*voice-over, from the skip*) Jo? Jo? What's going on out there? It sounds like World War Three's just broken out.
Jo (*to the skip*) I think it has! Vyvian's just on his way to beat the living daylights out of your beloved Beverley.
Fiona (*voice-over, from the skip*) Oh, shoot! Come on. We must go and stop him. However bad he is, he doesn't deserve that!

Janet enters behind Jo

Jo (*to the skip; urgently*) No, Fee! You must stay in there! Don't forget Janet!
Janet At your service, young lady.
Jo (*jumping and turning round, trying to hide the skip*) Ah! Janet! I mean Inspector. Any luck with Fiona yet?
Janet I think I may've just struck gold — in a manner of speaking.
Jo Oh, yes?
Janet Are you in the 'abit of carrying on conversations with inanimate objects, miss?
Jo (*not understanding*) I'm sorry?
Janet That theatrical skip just be'ind you. You seemed to be talking to it just now.
Jo (*seeing the skip as if for the first time*) What? Oh, this! Gosh! How did that get there?
Janet You seemed to address it as "Fee".
Jo Did I?
Janet That wouldn't be an affectionate abbreviation for "Fiona" by any chance, would it?
Jo Fiona? Oh, no, no, no. No, I was — (*thinking rapidly*) just — talking to the cheque I've just received for doing that advert.
Janet (*mystified*) Cheque, miss?

Act II

Jo Yes. I put it in this skip. "Stay in there, Fee," I said. "You'll be safe in there, Fee, until I take you to the bank tomorrow."
Janet (*having taken this in*) I see! So it's not your twin sister Fiona Smith 'iding inside that skip.
Jo Oh, no. (*Innocently pointing to the skip*) What, Fiona in here? No, no. Good heavens. No.
Janet A pity, that.
Jo In what way "a pity"?
Janet Well, I shall 'ave to be on my way soon ...
Jo Oh. Shame!
Janet And if I don't find Fiona before I go, I won't be able to give 'er the good news, will I?
Jo Thank heavens for that! (*Suddenly realizing what he's said*) Good news? What good news? I thought you were going to arrest her!
Janet (*amused*) Arrest 'er? Oh, no, no! Nothing like that. No. We've 'ad a bit of a coup with some of the pimps in this district, that's all. Got a few of them be'ind bars at last. I just wanted to let 'er know.

During the following, a loud banging is heard over the speakers, as if someone were trying to kick a door down

Beverley (*over the speakers, over the banging*) Keep out, you maniac! I won't let you in here.
Vyvian (*over the speakers, over the banging, muffled as if behind a door*) Not a chance, you devious bastard! I'm kicking this door down now.

There is loud crash over the speakers as the door is kicked down

Beverley (*over the speakers*) Oh my God!
Vyvian (*over the speakers*) There you are, you bastard. Let me get hold of you.
Beverley (*over the speakers*) Not if I can help it.

The sounds of a tussle come over the speakers. Janet's and Jo's ensuing dialogue is loud, to be heard over the tussle

Janet What in the name of thunder's going on out there?
Jo It's Beverley and Vyvian. In the lighting box. They've finally got together.
Beverley (*over the speakers*) Don't you come near me!
Vyvian (*over the speakers*) I'll do what I like, you bastard!
Jo Should we go and stop them hurting each other, do you think?
Janet Not on your life! Let them fight it out for themselves.

Jo What about brotherly love?
Janet Brotherly love, my arse! It was like this when we were kids, you know.
Vyvian (*over the speakers*) Stand still, Beverley, and let me hit you!
Beverley (*over the speakers*) Ooh! Viv! Not playing with your knife any more?
Vyvian (*over the speakers*) Absolutely not! I'm through with all of that! I'll teach you to take advantage of me!
Beverley (*over the speakers, having been grabbed*) Ah! Put me down! (*Having been dropped*) Ow!

There is the most almighty crash of thunder over the speakers and a flash of lightning

Mind the sound equipment!
Vyvian (*over the speakers*) I don't care about the bloody sound equipment! I just want to hit you!

There is the smack of someone being punched over the speakers

Beverley (*over the speakers, as he's hit*) Ah!

There is the crash of someone falling to the floor over the speakers

Janet Oh, Jupiter! I suppose I'd better go up there and see if 'e's all right.
Fiona (*voice-over, from the skip*) Bob! Beverley! What's happened to him? Is he all right?

Janet turns back to the skip in surprise, and hovers indecisively between the skip and the exit

Jo No. No, don't worry. I'll go and see what's happened to him. You stay here and give the good news to Fiona.
Janet Fiona?
Jo Yes, of course. She's inside the skip, isn't she? (*She turns to exit, then turns back*) Looking after that cheque.

Jo exits

Vyvian (*over the speakers, slapping Beverley's cheek*) Come on, Beverley, you bastard. Wake up now so that I can hit you again.

Fiona climbs out of the skip

Act II   65

Fiona (*climbing out of the skip*) It's no good! I've got to see what's happened.
Janet (*turning to her*) Ah. Miss Fiona Smith?
Fiona (*seeing him, warily*) Who wants to know?
Janet Detective Inspector Janet Jones, miss. From the Vice Squad.
Fiona Oh, shoot! (*She tries to climb back into the skip*)
Janet (*stopping her*) Now, now, miss. No need for all that. I just want to give you a little piece of good news.
Fiona (*still wary*) What good news is that, then?
Janet Are you acquainted at all with a certain shady gentleman sometimes known by the alias of Rosco Wilkins?
Fiona (*pulling her face*) Der! I should think I am! He only takes most of what I earn.
Janet Not any more, 'e don't. 'E's safely tucked away be'ind bars. Along with all the rest of 'is organization. And from the size of the book we're about to throw at 'im, I shouldn't think 'e'll be coming out from be'ind them for quite some time.
Fiona (*hardly able to believe it*) You mean, you've arrested him?
Janet You're a free woman, Miss Smith. I just thought I'd let you know — officially like. I 'eard on the grapevine you was thinking of calling it a day.
Jo (*over the speakers*) Oh, crikey, what a mess! (*Seeing Beverley*) Oh, God! Beverley! Vyvian, what've you done!
Vyvian (*over the speakers*) It's all right! I didn't hit him very hard!
Jo (*over the speakers*) Vyvian!
Vyvian (*over the speakers*) OK! OK! Don't panic. He's still breathing.
Jo (*over the speakers*) Only just! come on! give me a hand to get him back downstairs.
Vyvian (*over the speakers*) Oh, very well! Let me get hold of him.
Jo (*over the speakers*) Here. Let me take some of the weight as well. (*Impressed*) Ooh. Vyvian. You are strong!
Vyvian (*over the speakers, rakishly*) You're not so feeble yourself, Jo Smith. (*Back to business*) Here we go, then! Hup! Mind the door frame.

There is a bump over the speakers as Beverley's head evidently makes contact with the door frame

Fiona Do you think he'll be all right?
Janet Oh, right as rain, I shouldn't wonder. I've seen this sort of thing 'appen between those two numbskulls a dozen times before, I can tell you.
Fiona Have you?
Janet Not since they grew up and left 'ome, mind you.
Fiona Ah.
Janet Anyway, don't you go bothering your good self about those two nincompoops. You've got a whole new life ahead of you now, 'aven't you?

Fiona Yes. You're right. I have.
Janet I should clear out of this theatre as fast as you can, if I were you — and start getting on with it!
Fiona (*with newfound relish*) Leave this theatre? No fear! I'm staying put.
Janet You're not considering a new career treading the boards as well, are you?
Fiona Oh, no. Certainly not! You see, I've got a few choice words I want to say to young Mr Beverleybob — when he comes round. Fiancée indeed! I mean, how special can she be?
Janet I like the sparkle in your eye! You go right ahead and do what you feel you have to.
Fiona Thank you, Inspector. I shall!
Jo (*voice-over; off*) I'll see if I can find a cushion anywhere out here, Vyvian!
Fiona (*hurriedly*) That's Jo. I don't think I can face her just yet. I'd better hide again. (*She climbs back into the skip*) Do me a favour and don't let on to her I'm in here, will you?
Janet (*jovially*) 'Appy to oblige.
Fiona (*pulling the lid of the skip down on herself*) Thanks.
Janet (*to the skip*) And you can do one little favour in return for me, eh, miss?
Fiona (*voice-over, from the skip*) What's that, inspector?
Janet (*to the skip*) Don't mess up again, eh. You've got a great chance 'ere.
Fiona (*voice-over, from the skip*) Don't worry! I won't!

Jo enters

Jo Oh. Inspector.
Janet 'Ow's the wounded soldier?
Jo Lying down in one of the dressing-rooms. Groaning. Vyvian's just making sure he's all right. He sent me to find a cushion for his head.
Janet (*looking about*) No cushion 'ere, as far as I can see.
Jo I'm sure Vyvian'll manage. Did you speak to her? Fiona, I mean?
Janet Yes I did, thank you, miss. And most gratified she was too. I think she feels it's like a bit of a fresh start.
Jo Oh, that's fantastic. Where is she now?
Janet (*acting very badly*) She's not in the theatre any more. She's gone away.
Jo Gone away? Gone away where?
Janet (*acting very badly*) I'm not exactly sure.
Jo (*a bit disappointed*) Oh. Well — do you think I could catch her up?
Janet (*acting very badly*) Out of the question — I should say.
Jo Oh. That's a shame. I wanted to get her phone number.
Janet (*back on firmer ground*) Oh. Don't you 'ave it already, miss?
Jo No. No, I've never needed it before. I thought she could come and stay with me for a while. If she wanted to. Just till she sorts herself out.

Act II

Janet That's very 'ospitable of you, miss.
Jo *She's* got *my* number, I think. Perhaps she'll call me.
Janet I expect she'll get to 'ear about it one way or another. These things 'ave a funny way of being passed on.
Jo Yes. Right.
Janet Well — I must be on my way, too, now, miss, if you'll excuse me.
Jo Yes. Of course.
Janet Goodbye, miss.
Jo Goodbye, Inspector.
Janet (*turning to go and then stopping himself with an afterthought*) Oh, and by the way — just a little piece of advice, if I may.
Jo (*brightly*) Oh yes?
Janet I'd give up acting, if I were you.
Jo (*affronted*) What?
Janet Only two telly appearances in your career and no feel for Shakespeare? I don't think you're really cut out for it.

Jo isn't quite able to think what to say

That's my opinion, anyway. And I do speak as a leading light of the Crowthorne (*or local town*) Amateur Shakespeare Players. Very pleasant to meet you, miss. Goodbye.

Janet exits

Jo (*calling after him, angrily*) Goodbye to you, too! Everyone's a critic! He didn't say *why* everyone was talking about his Bottom, did he? (*Shouting after him*) I bet it was rubbish!

Vyvian enters into the face of the shout

Vyvian What's that, my dear? What's rubbish?
Jo Your brother's Bottom!
Vyvian (*after a brief thought*) I just don't think I'll even ask!
Jo How's Beverley? I haven't found a cushion yet.
Vyvian Never mind. I rolled up an old towel for him. He's lying there perfectly comfortably, snoring like a pig.
Jo (*not to Vyvian*) So, then. I suppose we've failed.
Vyvian (*puzzled*) Have we? Failed at what?
Jo I can kiss goodbye to that extra sixty quid.
Vyvian What sixty pounds? I'm not quite following this.
Jo (*to Vyvian*) It's getting fairly late, isn't it?
Vyvian (*looking at his watch*) Oh, yes. I suppose it is.

Jo You can call her whenever you like.
Vyvian Can I? Call who?
Jo You know — thingummybob. That fiancée woman.
Vyvian Oh! Yes! Cheryl!
Jo That's her! You can spill all the beans to her about Beverley and Fiona.
Vyvian (*with a glint*) Yes! Yes I can!
Jo Poor old Beverley. He did try so hard.
Vyvian And yet, on reflection, you know, I don't think I'll bother!
Jo (*not hearing him*) Not that they sounded a particularly well-matched couple to me, I must say. (*Suddenly realizing what he's said*) What?
Vyvian I said, "On reflection, I don't think I'll bother."
Jo (*outraged*) You don't think you'll bother? After the afternoon I've just had?
Vyvian It's been quite a revelation to me, this afternoon, I can tell you.
Jo It's been quite a revelation to me, too!
Vyvian All that black magic business was twisting me up. On the whole, you know, I don't think I'll let my petty fraternal jealousy prevent Beverley and Cheryl from enjoying their sad little lives.
Jo (*teasing*) Vyvian! This isn't the late flowering of brotherly love between the two of you, is it?
Vyvian (*affronted*) What? Between me and Beverley? No fear! Brotherly love, my ——
Jo (*interrupting him*) Yes, I think I get the idea!
Vyvian And I shall be resigning my chairmanship of the Wokingham (*or local town*) and District Sons of Satan Society as from next Sunday week.
Jo Why next Sunday week?
Vyvian It's the AGM.
Jo (*with a smile*) Oh. Right.
Vyvian I don't suppose you'd care to join me for a little cappuccino, would you?
Jo A cappuccino?
Vyvian I know a sandwich shop just over the road. I'm quite friendly with the man who runs it — he's almost like a brother to me!
Jo (*coyly*) Are you making a pass at me?
Vyvian (*archly*) Not at all! I just thought it might be a good opportunity for us to discuss the furtherance of your career.
Jo (*tempted*) You're despicable!
Vyvian Enchanted.
Jo But what about Beverley?
Vyvian What about him?
Jo Do you think he'll be all right — if we leave him lying in that dressing-room all on his own?
Vyvian Hell's bells, he'll be fine! Do you think the first thing he'll want to see when he comes round again is me?

Act II

Jo No. You're right. He's probably best left to himself.
Vyvian (*with a twinkle*) And afterwards, perhaps, you'd care to come back to my place for a little bite of supper.
Jo (*also with a twinkle*) Oh. Well. That would depend, wouldn't it?
Vyvian Would it? What would it depend on?
Jo On whether or not one of those exciting parts you've got in the pipeline turned out to be an exciting part for *me*.
Vyvian (*liking her style*) Oh. Well. Yes. I see what you mean.
Jo And do you think one of them might be? In the pipeline? And exciting? For me?
Vyvian Well … Yes — I think one of them might be.
Jo And might that particular exciting part in the pipeline for me be a starring one?
Vyvian (*impressed*) I should think it's almost certain.
Jo Fantastic! (*Seductively*) Oh. Vyvian?
Vyvian Yes, my dear?
Jo You haven't given up your dark side altogether, have you?
Vyvian My dark side?
Jo Yes.
Vyvian (*looking around himself*) Am I not lit?
Jo No! I mean, that bit of the night in you — that little touch of wickedness.
Vyvian (*wickedly*) Oh. Yes, I understand you. No, no! I expect I shall still find a few little outlets for it — as life goes on.
Jo (*joining in*) Oh. Good!
Vyvian (*starting to leave*) Let's get that cappuccino. (*Stopping himself*) Oh. Pause a second. I think I've just found one.
Jo Found one what?
Vyvian A little outlet ——
Jo (*smiling*) Oh, yes?
Vyvian — for my dark side.
Jo And what might that be?
Vyvian What do you think I've got in my pocket?
Jo (*enjoying the double entendre*) Well — I'm not really sure!
Vyvian Go on. Guess!
Jo Give me a clue.
Vyvian It's just dangling there.
Jo (*slightly disappointed*) Oh. Is it?
Vyvian Sparkling.
Jo Oh my God! Yes, of course! Beverley's necklace!
Vyvian And do you know something — I think I'm going to keep it!
Jo Vyvian!
Vyvian As a little compensation for the disappointment of losing Cheryl.
Jo (*teasingly*) Oh, do you! (*A thought*) You know, it's probably just as well.
Vyvian How do you mean?

Jo Well — the moment he gave it to her, she'd know for certain he'd got something to be guilty about.
Vyvian Poor old Beverley. Come on!
Jo I'm right behind you!

Vyvian and Jo exit

The stage is empty for a few moments

Eventually Beverley staggers on. He is still a bit woozy, and has a huge bruise on his cheek. He moves to the front of the stage

Beverley (*calling out*) Hallo! Hallo! Is anyone there? (*Getting no response*) Oh. God. They must've all gone.

The skip slowly opens behind Beverley and Fiona appears. During the following, she climbs out of the skip and moves down behind Beverley

Well, that's very nice, I must say. I really *could've* been dead, lying in that dressing-room. I could've breathed my last. Fat lot they'd've cared about it! (*A bit troubled*) Bloody strange dream. That aeroplane flying off into the sunset. I've no idea what that was all about.
Fiona (*right into his ear*) Hallo.
Beverley (*jumping*) Oh my God! (*Turning and seeing Fiona*) You scared the life out of me. (*Taking her in, and liking what he sees*) Hallo. (*Suddenly doubtful*) Er — which one are you, actually?
Fiona I'm Fiona. (*Pause*) I think. (*After thinking about it*) No. No, I am. I'm Fiona. I'm very pleased I'm Fiona.
Beverley (*smiling at her*) That's nice.
Fiona (*with a twinkle*) And you are … ?
Beverley What?
Fiona Are you Bob? Or are you Beverley? I'm very confused.
Beverley Oh. Yes. I see what you mean. I'm Beverley.
Fiona Are you?
Beverley Yes. To you, I am. Please call me Beverley.
Fiona (*seductively*) Beverley.
Beverley (*giving in*) Fiona.

They kiss. Beverley's mobile phone rings. He detaches himself from Fiona, who continues to kiss and fondle him throughout the following

(*Answering the phone*) Hallo? … (*Lightly*) Oh! Cheryl! Yes! Hallo! (*Jolly and matter-of-fact*) Did you have a nice time? … (*Obviously having been*

Act II

told that she didn't) Oh, was it? ... No, I know it was an awfully long time. ... Yes, I'm sure it must've been hell. ... Well, I'm looking forward to seeing you again as well ——

Fiona does something briefly painful to him in the course of her caresses

Ow! ... No. Nothing. I'm fine. I — just — got my leg at a bit of a funny angle. ... No. ... No, I'm not distracted at all.

Fiona's attention becomes a little more intense

Listen — Cheryl — to be perfectly honest with you — there's a little something I've got to tell you!

The Lights fade to Black-out

FURNITURE AND PROPERTY LIST

ACT I

On stage: Grand theatre curtains
Battered old step-stool
Lamps
Rope
Ladder
Other theatre fit-up equipment

Off stage: Dummy version of **Beverley**'s legs

Personal: **Jo**: watch, handbag containing mobile phone
Beverley: mobile phone, watch (worn throughout)
Vyvian: red handkerchief, knife

ACT II

On stage: Closed theatrical skip with open back, accessible through the theatre curtains

Personal: **Vyvian**: devil half-mask
Beverley: wallet with money, jewellery box containing necklace

LIGHTING PLOT

Practical fittings required: nil
Interior. The same throughout

ACT I

To open: General interior lighting

Cue 1	**Vyvian**: " ... the starring role!"	(Page 34)
	Black-out	

ACT II

To open: General interior lighting

Cue 2	**Beverley**: "Here's where they work the lights."	(Page 53)
	Black-out	
Cue 3	**Beverley**: "Oops!"	(Page 53)
	Bring up lights	
Cue 4	Crash of thunder	(Page 60)
	Flash of lightning	
Cue 5	Crash of thunder	(Page 64)
	Flash of lightning	
Cue 6	**Beverley**: "... I've got to tell you!"	(Page 71)
	Fade to black-out	

EFFECTS PLOT

In the original Rumpus Theatre Company production, everything spoken offstage when the actor was onstage was pre-recorded and played through a variety of carefully positioned speakers, including one behind the curtain for the skip. Indeed, everything spoken from inside the skip, whether the actor was onstage or not, was recorded, to keep the sound quality the same.

ACT I

Cue 1	**Jo**: "Hallo? Hallo?" **Beverley**'s *voice from back of auditorium:* "Hallo."	(Page 1)
Cue 2	**Jo**: "Oh. Hallo?" **Beverley**'s *voice from off L:* "Hallo."	(Page 1)
Cue 3	**Beverley**: "Come out if I need to." **Vyvian**'s *voice from off R; dialogue as p.13*	(Page 13)
Cue 4	**Beverley**: " ... a wicked glint in his eye!" **Vyvian**'s *voice from off R; dialogue as p.13*	(Page 13)
Cue 5	**Vyvian**: "Bob!" **Fiona**'s *voice from off stage; dialogue as p. 18*	(Page 18)
Cue 6	**Jo**: "Agh!" **Beverley**'s *voice from behind curtain; dialogue as p.33*	(Page 33)
Cue 7	**Vyvian**: "I'm out here, you wimp!" **Beverley**'s *voice from behind curtain; dialogue as p.33*	(Page 33)
Cue 8	**Vyvian**: "Well, at last you've found me." **Beverley**'s *voice from behind curtain; dialogue as p.33*	(Page 33)
Cue 9	**Vyvian**: "Do what?" **Beverley**'s *voice from behind curtain; dialogue as p.33*	(Page 33)
Cue 10	**Vyvian**: " ... for yourself, haven't you?" **Beverley**'s *voice from behind curtain; dialogue as p.33*	(Page 33)

Effects Plot

Cue 11	**Vyvian**: "Why don't you come out here?" **Beverley**'s *voice from behind curtain; dialogue as p.33*	(Page 33)
Cue 12	**Vyvian**: "Agh!" *Sounds of a fight, with the voices of* **Beverley** *and* **Vyvian** *as p. 33*	(Page 33)

ACT II

Cue 13	**Vyvian**: " … ripe for sacrifice!" **Jo**'s *voice from skip; dialogue as p.35*	(Page 35)
Cue 14	**Vyvian** moves about and hums. When ready **Jo**'s *voice from skip; dialogue as p.35*	(Page 35)
Cue 15	**Vyvian**: "I need to concentrate." **Jo**'s *voice from skip; dialogue as p.35*	(Page 35)
Cue 16	**Vyvian** moves about and hums. When ready **Jo**'s *voice from skip; dialogue as p.35*	(Page 35)
Cue 17	**Vyvian**: "What is it now?" **Jo**'s *voice from skip; dialogue as p.35*	(Page 35)
Cue 18	**Vyvian**: "Why Sunday?" **Jo**'s *voice from skip; dialogue as p.36*	(Page 36)
Cue 19	**Vyvian**: " … meeting of the society, you mean?" **Jo**'s *voice from skip; dialogue as p.36*	(Page 36)
Cue 20	**Vyvian**: "Acolytes. Attendant priests." **Jo**'s *voice from skip; dialogue as p.36*	(Page 36)
Cue 21	**Vyvian**: "I think — better not!" **Jo**'s *voice from skip; dialogue as p.36*	(Page 36)
Cue 22	**Vyvian**: "Don't you think so?" **Jo**'s *voice from skip; dialogue as p.36*	(Page 36)
Cue 23	**Vyvian**: "In what way 'left out'?" **Jo**'s *voice from skip; dialogue as p.36*	(Page 36)
Cue 24	**Vyvian**: " … a little bit shocking." **Jo**'s *voice from skip; dialogue as p.36*	(Page 36)
Cue 25	**Vyvian**: " … his actually being my brother." *Noise like raspberry comes from the skip*	(Page 38)

Cue 26	**Vyvian**: " ... I've been waiting for all my life!" *Raspberry from skip*	(Page 39)
Cue 27	**Vyvian**: " ... one glorious gesture of evil!" *Slightly more prolonged raspberry*	(Page 39)
Cue 28	**Jo**: "I know!" *Raspberry from skip*	(Page 39)
Cue 29	**Vyvian**: "It's got me all excited." *Raspberry from skip*	(Page 40)
Cue 30	**Vyvian**: "My stomach's gone all funny now!" *Raspberry from skip*	(Page 41)
Cue 31	**Jo**: "I'll have to check my diary." *Raspberry from skip*	(Page 41)
Cue 32	**Jo**: "You can cheer each other up!" *Raspberry from skip*	(Page 41)
Cue 33	**Jo**: "Ow! Mind my bum!" *Raspberry from skip*	(Page 41)
Cue 34	**Jo** hurries off *Loud feedback noise over the speakers,* *then dialogue and effects as p.53-54*	(Page 53)
Cue 35	**Jo**: " ... he's looking for the prostitute." **Fiona**'s *voice from off stage; dialogue as p. 55*	(Page 55)
Cue 36	**Vyvian** sits on the skip. Pause **Fiona**'s *voice from the skip; dialogue as p.56*	(Page 56)
Cue 37	**Vyvian**: "Yes." **Fiona**'s *voice from the skip; dialogue as p.56*	(Page 56)
Cue 38	**Vyvian**: "No, you don't." **Fiona**'s *voice from the skip; dialogue as p.56*	(Page 56)
Cue 39	**Vyvian**: "It's not me you love." **Fiona**'s *voice from the skip; dialogue as p.56*	(Page 56)
Cue 40	**Vyvian**: "Because I'm not Bob." **Fiona**'s *voice from the skip; dialogue as p.56*	(Page 56)
Cue 41	**Vyvian**: "I'm Bob's identical twin brother, Vyvian." **Fiona**'s *voice from the skip; dialogue as p.56*	(Page 56)

Effects Plot 77

Cue 42	**Vyvian**: "Yes." Pause **Fiona**'s *voice from the skip; dialogue as p.56*	(Page 56)
Cue 43	**Vyvian**: "Yes, that's me." **Fiona**'s *voice from the skip; dialogue as p.56*	(Page 56)
Cue 44	**Vyvian** does a thumbs-up sign **Fiona**'s *voice from the skip; dialogue as p.57*	(Page 57)
Cue 45	**Vyvian**: "What is it?" **Fiona**'s *voice from the skip; dialogue as p.57*	(Page 57)
Cue 46	**Vyvian**: "Does it?" **Fiona**'s *voice from the skip; dialogue as p.57*	(Page 57)
Cue 47	**Vyvian**: "That'll be the spirit." **Fiona**'s *voice from the skip; dialogue as p.57*	(Page 57)
Cue 48	**Vyvian**: "I've read all about it." **Fiona**'s *voice from the skip; dialogue as p.57*	(Page 57)
Cue 49	**Vyvian**: "Beverley's." **Fiona**'s *voice from the skip; dialogue as p.57*	(Page 57)
Cue 50	**Vyvian**: "I mean Bob's." **Fiona**'s *voice from the skip; dialogue as p.57*	(Page 57)
Cue 51	**Vyvian**: "Yes." **Fiona**'s *voice from the skip; dialogue as p.57*	(Page 57)
Cue 52	**Vyvian**:"And his spirit's out to get me." *Loud squeal over the speakers followed by* **Beverley**: "Oh, bugger!" *and then speakers click off*	(Page 57)
Cue 53	**Vyvian**: "There he is now!" **Fiona**'s *voice from the skip; dialogue as p.58*	(Page 58)
Cue 54	**Vyvian**: "He's coming to get me!" **Fiona**'s *voice from the skip; dialogue as p.58*	(Page 58)
Cue 55	**Vyvian** exits **Fiona**'s *voice from the skip; dialogue as p.58*	(Page 58)
Cue 56	**Jo**: "Oh, do be quiet, Fiona!" **Fiona**'s *voice from the skip; dialogue as p.58*	(Page 58)
Cue 57	**Jo**: "It's me. Jo." **Fiona**'s *voice from the skip; dialogue as p.58*	(Page 58)

Cue 58	**Jo**: "We didn't ask you to leave." **Fiona**'s voice from the skip; dialogue as p.58	(Page 58)
Cue 59	**Jo**: "No! Don't do that!" **Fiona**'s voice from the skip; dialogue as p.58	(Page 58)
Cue 60	**Jo**: "Here comes Janet now!" **Fiona**'s voice from the skip; dialogue as p.58	(Page 58)
Cue 61	**Jo**: "The Vice Squad officer!" **Fiona**'s voice from the skip; dialogue as p.58	(Page 58)
Cue 62	**Janet** exits. Pause **Fiona**'s voice from the skip; dialogue as p.59	(Page 59)
Cue 63	**Jo**: " … so don't move!" **Fiona**'s voice from the skip; dialogue as p.59	(Page 59)
Cue 64	**Jo**: "No, Fiona, he's not dead." **Fiona**'s voice from the skip; dialogue as p.59	(Page 59)
Cue 65	**Jo**: "What man from the sandwich shop?" **Fiona**'s voice from the skip; dialogue as p.59	(Page 59)
Cue 66	**Jo**: " … in that loo just now?" **Fiona**'s voice from the skip; dialogue as p.59	(Page 59)
Cue 67	**Jo**: "… for about twenty minutes." **Fiona**'s voice from the skip; dialogue as p.59	(Page 59)
Cue 68	**Jo**: " Well — anyway — he's not!" **Fiona**'s voice from the skip; dialogue as p.59	(Page 59)
Cue 69	**Jo**: " … come to think of it!" **Fiona**'s voice from the skip; dialogue as p.59	(Page 59)
Cue 70	**Jo**: " … not ten minutes ago." **Fiona**'s voice from the skip; dialogue as p.59	(Page 59)
Cue 71	**Jo**: "Janet's still on the warpath, remember?" **Fiona**'s voice from the skip; dialogue as p.59	(Page 59)
Cue 72	**Jo**: "His name's Beverley really." **Fiona**'s voice from the skip; dialogue as p.59	(Page 59)
Cue 73	**Jo**: " … so all you girls won't make fun of him." **Fiona**'s voice from the skip; dialogue as p.60	(Page 59)

Effects Plot 79

Cue 74   **Jo**: " And he's engaged as well."   (Page 60)
         Fiona's *voice from the skip; dialogue as p.60*

Cue 75   **Jo**: " … better off without him."   (Page 60)
         Fiona *wails from the skip*

Cue 76   **Jo**: " … back at home to Mum and Dad."   (Page 60)
         Fiona's *voice from the skip; dialogue as p.60*

Cue 77   **Jo**: " … sort something out between us."   (Page 60)
         Beverley's voice over the speakers; dialogue as p. 60

Cue 78   **Jo**: " Yes, Beverley. It's me."   (Page 60)
         Fiona's *voice from the skip; dialogue as p.60*

Cue 79   **Jo**: "This should put you off him forever."   (Page 60)
         Beverley's *voice over the speakers; dialogue as p. 60*

Cue 80   **Jo**: "No, I'm Jo all right."   (Page 60)
         Beverley's *voice over the speakers; dialogue as p. 60*

Cue 81   **Jo**: "Oh! Fantastic!"   (Page 60)
         Beverley's *voice over the speakers; dialogue as p. 60*

Cue 82   **Jo**: " … shut away safely in the loo."   (Page 60)
         Beverley's *voice over the speakers; dialogue as p. 60.*
         Then almighty crash of thunder over the speakers.
         Pause. Then **Beverley**'s *voice; dialogue as p. 60*

Cue 83   **Jo**: " … not scare him half to death."   (Page 60)
         Beverley's *voice over the speakers; dialogue as p. 60*

Cue 84   **Jo**: " … Scooby Doo would be too much!"   (Page 60)
         Beverley's *voice over the speakers; dialogue as p. 60*

Cue 85   **Jo**: "He's barking!"   (Page 61)
         Fiona's *voice from the skip; dialogue as p.61*

Cue 86   **Jo**: "You're barking as well!"   (Page 61)
         Beverley's *voice over the speakers; dialogue as p. 61*

Cue 87   **Jo**: "I'm going as fast as I can."   (Page 61)
         Beverley's *voice over the speakers; dialogue as p. 61*

Cue 88   **Jo**: "I gave it back to you."   (Page 61)
         Beverley's *voice over the speakers; dialogue as p. 61*

Cue 89	**Jo**: "Yes I did." **Beverley**'s *voice over the speakers; dialogue as p. 61*	(Page 61)
Cue 90	**Jo**: "I gave it to Vyvian by mistake." **Beverley**'s *voice over the speakers; dialogue as p. 61*	(Page 61)
Cue 91	**Jo**: "Yes. Sorry. I thought he was you." **Beverley**'s *voice over the speakers; dialogue as p. 61*	(Page 61)
Cue 92	**Jo**: "I didn't do it on purpose." **Beverley**'s *voice over the speakers; dialogue as p. 61*	(Page 61)
Cue 93	**Vyvian**: " ... everything you've just said." **Beverley**'s *voice over the speakers; dialogue as p. 61*	(Page 61)
Cue 94	**Vyvian**: " ... the dead to get me ——" **Beverley**'s *voice over the speakers; dialogue as p. 61*	(Page 61)
Cue 95	**Vyvian**: " ... coming up there to get you!" **Beverley**'s *voice over the speakers; dialogue as p. 61*	(Page 61)
Cue 96	**Jo**: "Oh! Thanks!" **Beverley**'s *voice over the speakers; dialogue as p. 62*	(Page 62)
Cue 97	**Vyvian** exits **Beverley**'s *voice from speakers; dialogue as p. 62*	(Page 62)
Cue 98	**Jo**: "He's still got that knife." **Fiona**'s *voice from the skip; dialogue as p. 62*	(Page 62)
Cue 99	**Jo**: " ... out of your beloved Beverley!" **Fiona**'s *voice from the skip; dialogue as p. 62*	(Page 62)
Cue 100	**Janet**: "I just wanted to let 'er know." *Banging, dialogue from* **Beverley** *and* **Vyvian**, *crash and tussle over speakers as p. 63*	(Page 63)
Cue 101	**Jo**: "They've finally got together." **Beverley**'s *and* **Vyvian**'s *voices over the speakers;* *dialogue as p. 63*	(Page 63)
Cue 102	**Janet**: " ... when we were kids, you know." **Vyvian**'s *and* **Beverley**'s *voices over the speakers,* *crash of thunder, smack and crash as p. 64*	(Page 64)
Cue 103	**Janet**: " ... and see if 'e's all right." **Fiona**'s *voice from the skip; dialogue as p. 62*	(Page 64)

Effects Plot 81

Cue 104	**Jo** exits **Vyvian**'s *voice over the speakers; dialogue as p. 64*	(Page 64)
Cue 105	**Janet**: "… you was thinking of calling it a day." *Dialogue from* **Jo** *and* **Vyvian** *over the speakers as p.65, followed by bump*	(Page 65)
Cue 106	**Fiona**: "Thank you, Inspector, I shall." **Jo**'s *voice over the speakers; dialogue as p. 66*	(Page 66)
Cue 107	**Janet**: " … in return for me, eh, miss?" **Fiona**'s *voice from the skip; dialogue as p. 65*	(Page 66)
Cue 108	**Janet**: "You've got a great chance 'ere." **Fiona**'s *voice from the skip; dialogue as p. 65*	(Page 66)
Cue 109	**Fiona** and **Beverley** kiss **Beverley**'s *mobile phone rings*	(Page 70)